J Stephen Sadler's Quest For The Best

Bringing Fine Dining To Small Town America

The Challenges of Becoming an Entrepreneur in America

J Stephen Sadler

Copyright© 2021 by Sadler Media, LLC

All Rights Reserved. No part of this book maybe used, reproduced or transmitted in any form or by any means, electronic or mechanical, including photocopying, recording or by any information storage and retrieval system without permission in writing from the author.

Published by Sadler Media, LLC

Printed in the United States of America

ISBN: 978-1-953578-18-1

Library of Congress: 2021905132

Follow him on social media @ jstephensadler

www.sadler.media

DEDICATION

This book is dedicated to my dad who taught me that I could do anything I wanted if I wanted it bad enough. Without his guidance and the tenacity and hutzpah he instilled in me, I would never have had the belief in myself to think I could become a restauranteur with absolutely no experience whatsoever.

TABLE OF CONTENTS

Page 9	Forward
Page 11	In The Beginning
Page 12	Easy Peasy
Page 15	Introducing My Family Heirloom
Page 17	Morphing Into A Vision
Page 20	A Costly Lesson
Page 22	Fate Awakens a Calling
Page 24	A Cottage Industry Start
Page 27	Finding A Place That Would Fit
Page 31	3-Steps To A Vibrant Downtown
Page 35	If You Build It, They Will Come
Page 41	It's All In The Details
Page 48	The Birth of a Dream
Page 52	A Bistro Unlike Any Other
Page 58	It's All In The Experience
Page 62	We're Having A Party
Page 68	Hello, Let Me Introduce Myself
Page 73	Building a Website... The Long Winding Road to Nowhere
Page 77	How We Use Social Networks
Page 82	Where... What... When
Page 88	Luck... I Don't Think So!!
Page 91	Considering a Culinary Arts School... Maybe Not!
Page 94	Hiding The Bake House

Page 96	Staffing…The Real Challenge
Page 107	Branding - Deciding Who We Are
Page 111	Being Good Citizens of Our Pale Blue Dot
Page 115	Crumbzz Chocolate Sustainable Farming Goal Hits 100%!
Page 118	Saving Our Planet, One Meal At a Time
Page 121	Creating a Differentiator
Page 124	A Sampling of Some Common Dishes We Made Uniquely Uncommon
Page 124	How To Craft A Better Egg
Page 129	Searching The World For A Better Waffle
Page 132	More Old Favorites and Something New
Page 138	Chasing The Sun
Page 140	Europe
Page 142	North America
Page 143	South America
Page 144	Asia
Page 144	Carribean / Central America
Page 146	The Quest Goes On
Page 148	Q&A With Chef J Stephen
Page 198	J Stephen's Actual To Do List
Page 198	Legal/Financial/Licensing
Page 204	Vendor Procurement
Page 224	Branding/Packaging
Page 241	Marketing/Public Relations/Sales
Page 264	Accounting/Operations/Staffing
Page 285	About The Author

FORWARD

Finding his cafe in New York to be too much of a time and labor commitment had motivated Chef J Stephen Sadler to sell and move to the Dallas, Texas area where he happily slid into what he liked to call a "Regular Nine to Fiver Guy" position. But, a chance encounter, Karma and a family recipe that failed to die had other plans.

Quest For The Best...Bringing Fine Dining To Small Town America is a story of a family heirloom that, like a phoenix, refused to be forgotten and how this little family recipe combined with his world travels led him to bring fine dining dishes from across the world to small town America.

The challenges faced by what he called a "novice at every turn" in starting a fine dining restaurant from scratch in small town America would easily have been insurmountable to most people. But the "you can do anything if you really want to" mindset his father had taught him burned so fiercely within that he refused to walk away from the many setbacks that would have told a sane person to walk away.

Why, who, where and how, we're all questions he had to answer on a daily basis. **Why** was he doing this? He hated how his place in New York consumed his entire life. Was it for the money, the challenge or something much deeper? **Who** would actually dine at a fine dining restaurant that featured dishes from across the world, dishes that were about as far away from the traditional meat and potatoes diets of most small town America diners? **Where** would be the best location to test his theory that small town America, if offered something different, would be interested in more than just their normal meat and potatoes every day fare? **How** could he pull this all together. He had never built a restaurant from scratch, crafted a menu of dishes he had enjoyed during his worldwide travels from scratch and do it all without borrowing money or taking on partners?

This is the story of how it all started, the challenges he faced, the failures and the successes that would eventually lead to one of the most unique bistros in America.

Quest For The Best...Bringing Fine Dining To Small Town America is the second book in the series. It is a great read not only for would be restaurateurs and those interested in remaking their life – but also anyone who loves to read a success story driven by a passion to honor a family's history.

IN THE BEGINNING

"It seemed so easy. rent a place...buy equipment...hire staff... advertise...wait for the crowds! That was the basic idea. The reality was anything but!"

"Becoming a restauranteur was not as simple as following the book on opening a restaurant from A to Z, it was more like following A to Z in a long lost language!"

Easy Peasy

    My older brother Ken and I had decided that we were going to open a deli in 1999. I can't recall whose idea it was or why we chose a deli over any other business we had no knowledge of but, a deli it was and so we set about planning our strategy.
    We had no experience in the food industry whatsoever but, coming from the same father who instilled in us that we could do whatever we wanted if we wanted it bad enough, we blindly went about looking for a deli to purchase. We would pool our funds, he would handle the front and I would handle the kitchen. Seemed pretty simple to us. An ongoing business that we could just slot ourselves into, as we found our way easily learning the food business as we went.
    After several month's of searching, we found a deli to our liking in a cute little town in the Hudson Valley area of New York State. Highland Falls was a sleepy little one traffic light town inhabited by commuters who would get

on the train or bus every morning and dutifully head into the city to work at their jobs and then return every night to their loved ones.

Our targeted deli was always busy serving those commuters as they came and went in the mornings and afternoons and their families during the days and on weekends. everything seemed perfectly ideal!

And so, we jumped in...kind of. We would not only buy the business but also the building that housed it. This way we would be in complete control of our own destiny. At the time, my brother was in the process of purchasing a home and did not want to complicate his purchase by applying for another loan for our business. And so, I signed for our loan. You know what's coming don't you. Well, I'm glad you do because I didn't. Two weeks before we were to close, my brother decided that being in the deli business was not what he wanted to do after all and backed out of the deal. And so it was now my deal! Was I to go through with it by myself? Could I handle it alone? This is where my dad's creed that "we could do whatever we wanted if we wanted it bad enough" came back to bite me in the you know where.

Of course, I figured I could handle this on my own and so, the papers were signed, the money changed hands and I was the proud owner of a deli... my own deli! Well, not really on my own because I soon discovered why the original owners were two instead of one. My deli experience would not only include me but my wife (who happened to have her own job as a teacher) AND my two boys!

I quickly learned that owning a deli, as with all restaurants, was an all encompassing affair. Yes I had all my dishes already set, my suppliers in place, my employees hired but, there were so many things I needed be prepared to do on a daily basis that it took all of my waking hours just to get through the day. It was my first experience with the term "trial by fire!" One thing ran through my head on a daily basis. When I had asked the previous owners why they were selling they said "To HAVE A LIFE". It was funny at the time. It was only after I purchased my little deli that I realized it was prophetic!

My learning curve was high and although I had written into my deal that the previous owners had to stay to teach me the business for two month's, I soon realized that I should have required them to stay for two years!

Owning a restaurant whether it be a deli, coffee shop, fine dining or fast food is unlike owning any other business. You not only have your employees to deal with but also the requirement to prepare, on a daily basis, everything you sell. Think of a clothing store who has to create, from scratch, on a daily basis, all the clothing they are selling! In addition, unlike a clothing store, gift shop or other retail store, if you don't sell your product on a daily basis, you throw it away! Now add to that the multitude of licensing and inspection requirements as well as equipment that needs constant upkeep that you don't have with any other retail store and you get some idea of the challenges you face.

Nevertheless, I ever so slowly learned what it was like to own a business that served food to the public.

Introducing My Family Heirloom

Cakers waiting for their slice of Crumbzz cake

Although not as common in the rest of the country, in New York, deli's are everywhere. My deli offered the standard fare of cold cuts, salads, sandwiches, beer and wine. In addition, half of the deli was stocked with groceries, making it kind of like a little farm store.

We were also known not only for its unique sandwiches but also our great pies and cakes as well as our many pastries, all made from scratch. This is the part of the deli I was most interested in. This is where I planned to introduce my family's Crumbzz artisan crumb cake.

We offered four flavors, chocolate, apricot, raspberry and the original cinnamon streusel. Within a few month's, we started to have lines form outside our door awaiting our freshly made Crumbzz artisan crumb cakes, hot from the oven. Commuters would grab a slice and a coffee to take on their commute into the city. Our Crumbzz artisan crumb cake sales became so popular that we had to extend our opening hours so that the "cakers" as they were now being called, would not miss their ride into the city.

As our cakes became ever more popular, we began to have people drive from the city to our little deli to purchase cakes to take back home. At our height, we were selling 50-70 sheet trays of cakes (24 slices to a tray) every day!

Eventually, we began to get requests to ship our cakes across the country. Shipping cakes was not something I wanted to do because I had already begun to remove chemicals, preservatives or artificial flavorings from my offerings (a thing that was quite unusual at that time) and could not guarantee they would get to their destination and still remain fresh. You need to understand that at this time, FedEx was not a thing and the Internet was not used to buy anything. I nonetheless, did begin to ship cakes and by 2002, we shipped approximately 500 cakes. That sounds small now but, at the time it was quite impressive.

This was the beginning of offering my family's 400-year old Crumbzz Cake (as I was now calling it) to the public, and it had become a rousing success.

Little did I know that in the years to come, it would become the driving force behind everything I did.

Morphing Into a Vision

The family artisan crumb cakes were first reborn at J Stephen's Upstate New York Home

As I mentioned in the previous chapter, it was the many pastries, cakes and pies that had interested me the most. I was never really interested in cooking. I know that sounds funny coming from a chef but, you need to understand that chef's fall into two categories; pastry chefs (bakers) and savory chefs (cooks). One is right brain and one is left. I would often chuckle when a new chef would tell me they do both, because, as a chef you may be able to DO both but, you will eventually end up being (based on your brain type) either a pastry chef OR a savory chef. It is so pronounced that I had every "potential" chef I considered hiring participate in my Personality Profile Seminar (a program that I had been teaching on the side for years) to understand exactly which type of chef I was hiring.

Savory chefs are more a splash of this and a dash of that type of people. They adjust as they go and are often imprecise in their measurements (can you say a cup of flour). On the other hand, pastry chefs are like chemists, precisely measuring each ingredient because, unlike cooking, once you place your cake, pie or pastry in the oven there is no adjustments, no going back. Remember that cup of flour I mentioned previously for the savory chef? Well, a pastry chef would NEVER use a "cup" of flour! They would instead measure out 4 1/4 ounces of flour, utilizing a scale.

Back to my pastries, we sold a lot of pastries at my little bakery-deli (which was how we were now known). In fact we made over 60 different pastries, cakes and pies on a daily basis and that didn't even include my Crumbzz artisan crumb cakes! Now that might sound like a lot of pastries, cakes and pies to most, but in the New York area, that was a pretty standard mix for a bakery. I always laugh at the "bakeries" I find in Dallas which usually offer wedding cakes, cookies and cupcakes. THAT'S not a bakery by any standard I know!

As with most bakeries, we sold enormous amounts of baked goods during the holiday season, which included Easter, Thanksgiving and Christmas. Interestingly, Easter was when we sold the most cakes, Thanksgiving the most pies and Christmas the most pastries.

As I expanded our baking, I also eliminated our grocery sales and converted that area into a cafe. Once I had the cafe up and running, I added wine and beer by the glass and expanded our hours to include the evenings. Our cafe became the in place to be in the evenings and within a year surpassed my deli sales.

Little did I realize that the success of the changes I had made would eventually drive me out of the business.

As the winter of 2010 set in, I experienced what is commonly known as "burnout." In all honesty, I'm sure it being winter also helped bring on my burnout. You see, even though I was born and raised in the New York area, I always hated the cold. To me, winters are something you put up with while desperately holding on for Spring to arrive. But winter may have contributed to my burnout but, I knew clearly what was the main cause.

In any business, especially the restaurant business, in order to be successful, the owner MUST be on the premises. The business takes on the owners personality (good or bad) and NO ONE can replace that. You may not need an on-site owner for fast food because its, speed and price that are the driving factors but, in the fine dining business, the owners presence can often make the difference between success or failure. And so, I remained a prisoner to my own creation.

I can't say that I didn't take some time off but, it was always hours, never days. With hours of 7 am - 10 pm 7-days a week, I would come home, eat, go to bed, get up and go to work. My wife helped out whenever she could and my youngest son would often cover for me on some of the evenings but, the hours eventually took their toll until one incident occurred which would be the eventual catalyst that moved me to make a life-changing decision.

My oldest son who was in college, came home to visit us on Memorial Day of 2011. As a surprise, he offered to give me the day off as he would cover for me on a holiday that, because people sleep in on holidays, should be quiet. Since he had worked off and on when he could at our now bakery/cafe (as it was now called), I thought that would be a wonderful gift. However, one hour after he opened, I received a desperate phone call. The only word I could understand was "HELP!" My lovely bride and I as well as my youngest son threw on our clothes and rushed to our little "quiet" place of business. What we found was a line a mile long. Need I say, we all worked our tales off that day and didn't stop until we locked the doors! That was all I needed to push me into selling as soon as I could.

A Costly Lesson

The sale of my business was complicated by several factors that simultaneously came into play. Knowing that we were selling, my wife had taken a teaching position in our eventual destination of Dallas, TX. My youngest son has been accepted into Texas Tech (as the name implies, also in Texas) which left me all alone to deal with the pressures of operating while selling my business. In addition, I was also in the process of selling my home. All that was left in New York was my trusty dog and I. As September rolled in, the weather was beginning to change into its fall foliage (which, unlike everyone else, I never enjoyed because it was a sure sign that winter was not far behind). To add to these complications, that was the year of 911, that terrible loss that turned everyones world upside down. In the middle of all this, I was growing more weary of my time (now alone) trudging to and from what was now my personal prison.

Restaurants are not an easy business to sell. They are complicated to run, hard to quantify and require a person that loves the art of cooking/baking but also has the smarts to run such a complicated business. Since this business was my baby (prison or not) it took several month's to find what I believed to be the best "qualified" buyer. I finally found a Greek restaurant owner who matched what I thought was my requirements and who was qualified to buy my business. The only outstanding issue was how he was going to pay for it.

I wanted to be paid out in full and he wanted to finance with 10% down. Normally, that would have been a deal breaker for me but, because of all the complications mentioned above, I acquiesced and accepted his offer. Whether that was a mistake or not is hard to say because of where I eventually ended up but, it clearly wasn't a smart business move. Having sold my house, my dog and I were living in a hotel room for the last 30-days of my stay in New York. Not a pleasant occurrence for her, me or, I'm sure, the hotel. But, we packed up our belongings hopped in the car and headed south to Dallas. Fittingly, as we drove out of New York, winter made its last statement to me as snow began to fall. It was the most beautiful snow I had ever seen... because it would be the last one I would see!

Of course you know the end of this chapter in my life. That Greek restaurant owner, completely changed my restaurant over to a Greek restaurant, defaulted on his loan to me and promptly went out of business. Why he purchased my restaurant and then converted it into a Greek restaurant is beyond my understanding. Wouldn't it have been better to just start from scratch and open a Greek restaurant? When he defaulted I had a choice, go back up and salvage what I could or walk away. With my family and new home now all in Texas, my business gutted and a shell of what it once was, I chose the latter. It was a lesson I learned the hard way that I would pay for for many years thereafter but, it was a lesson well learned. I put away my family recipe, my interest in owning a restaurant and any desire to bake for years. It was time to move on. That was until fate would once again play a hand in changing my life.

Fate Awakens a Calling

Chef J Stephen in his kitchen

When I sold my company, I sold everything BUT my family's Crumbzz artisan crumb cake recipe. For seven years, our "family famous" little Crumbzz artisan crumb cake became a wonderful, but distant memory. That is until fate once again would intervene in my life.

The airport in Dallas know as DFW Airport is big. How big? It is the same size as Manhattan! That I would run into someone from my New York days were infinitesimally small but, that is exactly what happened. As I was running to catch a plane I felt a tap on the back. The person tapping said "J Stephen, how the hell are you"? I remember thinking at the time that, this must be how it feels to have Alzheimers, since I had no earthly idea who this stranger was. Unbelievably, he was an old customer from my New York cafe days who now lived in

Oklahoma City who often came down to Dallas to catch a plane to visit his clients across the U.S.

That I would run into an old NY customer, who now lived in Oklahoma, in of all places, my new home of Dallas, just add's to the story of how my family Crumbzz artisan crumb cake simply refused to die.

Stories of the days in Highland Falls eventually got around to those famous Crumbzz artisan crumb cakes and the customer asked if I would bake a special crumb cake just for him. I didn't promise him anything, since I was no longer in the cake making business but I took his home information as a courtesy.

Although that passing encounter was a pleasant surprise, I still had no intention of resurrecting my family heirloom. That is until my return home and subsequent discussion with my lovely bride of thirty plus years.

My wife Catherine pointed out that it was not inconsequential that I had signed a seven year no complete with the buyers of my deli/cafe in New York and even though they defaulted which probably nullified my agreement, that I had run into an old customer seven years after I had sold was not merely a coincidence. I am a firm believer in karma and that was as close to karma as I needed to come to receive the sign. The memories of my business sale disaster had long dissipated and I had to admit that it was an intriguing thought to pull out my family recipe and see if I still had the touch.

Finding my old recipe was a real challenge, but I eventually located it in a dusty old box in my attic. From there it was like riding a bike, once I started, it all came naturally.

Years after the recipe was lost under a pile of dust, I once again started creating our "once famous" Crumbzz cakes, along with a new twist that became the talk of North Texas.

A Cottage Industry Start

The Sadler "Cottage Bakery" Home

Having "retired" from the restaurant and baking business that I owned in New York and not touched a single kitchen utensil for several years, I knew that starting over again was not going to be a walk in the park. I was now in a new town in the mid-west. I knew I would be dealing with people who had new tastes and different dining experiences than those in New York. What worked in New York would not necessarily work in Dallas, Texas. But, I was going to market my family heirloom cakes online and that would mean a much bigger market than simply Dallas.

Knowing the hours required and staffing challenges that were part and parcel with any restaurant, I had NO intention of opening a retail operation whatsoever. I also knew it would be smart to start small and ramp up as I saw fit. And so I decided to begin making my family Crumbzz artisan crumb cakes from my home in what one would call a "Cottage Industry" start up. To do this, I knew I would need to update my lovely brides kitchen. Having worked in a commercial kitchen had spoiled me and taught me that it took the right tools (and appliances) to do the job right.

And so, I went about purchasing a new oven. It had to be convection to assure my cakes came out the same way, every time. Once I had purchased my oven, I moved on to a new microwave which would need to be larger and more powerful than a conventional home microwave. I would need at least 2000 watts of power to handle what I planned to do. Next was the purchase of a large commercial refrigerator and a multitude of small hand appliances, including tabletop mixers and food processors and finally I would need to replace our kitchen sink.

I've always hated the common double sinks found in most home kitchens and we had one in our kitchen as well. How you can do ANYTHING in a double sink, is beyond me. Contrary to what you might assume my wife was not averse to my upgrading "her" kitchen. She LOVED her new oven, micro and especially her new large single basin sink. And so, we were on our way to cottage baking at it's finest. I had anticipated everything, or so I thought, and was ready to get going. The beginning of my cake business would start right out of my house.

My Pack & Ship Area (Dining Room)

Although my kitchen was now the perfect setup to start my new venture, the rest of my home was not. We lived in a small cottage type home in an old area of Dallas. Our house was not even 1500 square feet and it quickly became obvious that as the orders started rolling in and the cakes started rolling out, we needed space to store supplies and incoming products and outgoing cakes for delivery.

As our "little" cottage business grew, the orders kept multiplying. We were shipping 40-50 cakes at a time with little or no space to store the ingredients or finished products. Our little guest room became the production room where the ingredients were stored and mixed. Bags of flour, sugar, cinnamon and spices shared this room with our two mixers bowls, paddles and other production tools. Our kitchen became the bakery with unbaked cakes, filed in their molds coming in and freshly baked cakes, going out. Our dining room became the packaging and shipping room with packing material, boxes piled high to the roof and finished cakes completely covering our (once) dining table. There was little to no room to get from one place to the other.

I knew I had a capacity problem but wanted to keep my little "cottage business" little for as long as I could. Although it was obvious that my business had now outgrown our home, it wasn't until my Irish Setter decided to share in the enjoyment of eating some of my cakes that were sitting in my "staging" area, that I finally decided it was time to separate our living quarters from our business.

The Cake Thief awaiting his next delicacy

Finding A Place That Would Fit

In choosing a home for our commercial bake house, I wanted to make sure we took the environment into mind. Saving an old building from destruction would be preferable to building new. Setting up shop in an old part of town would be more desirable than building out in a modern strip center.

I always had visions of building an environmentally advanced facility that would be a "green" showcase. Unfortunately, as a start up, our budget would not allow us to create the green baking environment I envisioned.

I found several areas that had old buildings that I felt we could fit into nicely. However, we ran into an issue that stymied our attempts to find a home in any one of these buildings.

As I researched these locations, we ran into a deal killer disguised in the name of progress. Like many cities, Dallas has its share of old buildings in need of a little bit of loving to bring them back to life.

Unfortunately, also like most cities, Dallas' zoning requirements eliminate any hope of a start up doing just that. You see, Dallas requires that a building be "brought up to code" in any location that has been sitting vacant for over six months.

That included just about EVERY old building in the Dallas area that met our criteria.

Being "brought up to code" is an expensive proposition that includes installing sprinkler systems, grease drains, venting hoods, etc. We estimated that the cost to bring one of these old buildings "up to code" would cost us approximately $80K.

Spending $80K before we even installed equipment and finished out the space was not something I was prepared to do. I would much rather spend those funds on client support, product development and marketing.

I could find new locations in strip centers that were already "up to code" but part of our green mission included rehabilitating old structures not encouraging another strip center. And so my search went on.

On my many property scouting trips across the DFW Metroplex, in the Cedars area, just south of downtown Dallas, I continually passed a grand old hotel called the Ambassador Park. This beautiful hotel had lay vacant but was clearly cared for. The grounds were immaculately kept and the building, although obviously closed, seemed in excellent condition. On each trip, I would stop by to see if anyone was there. In each case I was met with silence. No answer at the door, no telephone number, nothing.

Online, I found that the hotel was a historic monument in a town that has so few. Built in 1904 in Sullivanesque skyscraper style, it was renovated in 1932 to reflect the local interest in Spanish Colonial Revival.

As the city's first suburban luxury hotel, it entertained presidents and royalty and was the first hotel west of the Mississippi to have an elevator. In 1965 it was recorded as a Texas Historical Landmark.

It had laid vacant for several years, and to me, cried out for some attention.

The more I researched, the more I felt this grand old lady fit with my vision perfectly. What better way to serve our earth friendly principles than to reawaken a sleeping beauty.

On my fifth trip to the hotel, I struck gold! A trip to the basement door resulted in a face-to-face encounter with the Ambassador's caretaker, a gentleman named Bill Holdeman. One conversation led to another, which led to my vision of saving an old building and bringing her back to life, which led to a tour of the grand old lady.

Like those old movies, where mysteriously, everything remains but the people, The Ambassador was a trip back in time. Its lobby still shone from the light of its majestic chandelier, its wide hallways with ceiling fans and plush carpeting hark back to a time when travel was a leisurely experience to be savored. Its two bedroom suites were still as they were back when guests would arrive from around the country. Beds neatly made, curtains drawn, standing ready for their next visitor.

The more I toured, the more I fell in love with this grand old lady.

My tour of its magnificent kitchen was more than I could have ever hoped for. Fully functional, with every appliance a commercial kitchen would need, I could feel the energy of its once large staff quickly setting about to service its restaurant and many guests.

From that point forward, I knew this would be our home. We would set up shop and bring life back to her old bones. Crumbzz at the Ambassador, a marriage of necessity, for both of us, but a marriage made in heaven, nonetheless. I signed our lease in April of 2009 and set up shop.

The beauty of working at first along and eventually with my team of six to bring life back to a grande old dame, was beyond compare. Every morning our team would enter through her beautiful lobby, down her spacious hallways into her once bustling kitchen to work our craft. Each evening, we would turn off the lights and bid her our fair adieu only to return the next day to fill her kitchen with the wonderful smells of fresh cakes, fresh from the oven, just like she experienced in her prime.

Our stay at the majestic Ambassador was not limited to our team alone. During our stay, we witnessed a marriage, two school graduations and a heartfelt departure of one of the care takers children to college. The caretaker's son became our little helper, always by my side whenever the "killer" mixers (as he called them) went on. We made new friends with this small group of a select fortunate few that were privileged to share living and working space in this special historic lady, a building that was exclusively our small groups to share. For whatever reason, it just felt right to craft cakes from the past, from a grand old hotel from the past. What could be more natural.

We would ply our craft at this lovely lady for one wonderful year and felt privileged to have had the opportunity to bring her back to life with a cake that had its own piece of history. But I realized that one thing was always missing. One thing that I, as a highly social person needed, was interaction with my clientele. Working in the Ambassador left me adrift from my client base and I knew I needed that interaction not only for my own well being but also to chart how we were doing in servicing our clientele. And so, I started looking for a retail space to serve the public on a daily basis. Not a full-blown restaurant mind you, just simple storefront to my bakery. As with every well thought out plan, that's not what would eventually happen.

3-Steps To A Vibrant Downtown

Before I committed to a space for my new retail location, I wanted a city that actually would work together with me to assure "OUR" success. I use the word "OUR" because MY success would be the city's success as well. Many cities simply don't get that dynamic.

Most cities want to have a vibrant, destination downtown. Few find the keys to succeed in that goal. Why? One of the reasons is how they look at the problem. As a member of several downtown business associations, I participated in many city downtown re-vitalization discussion groups. The common theme on the posts is one of regulation. Clean it up and they will come...in droves.

It's understandable that, as a public servant, city personnel's first inclination is to respond to the challenge based on what they have been trained to do best...regulate. But you can't regulate your way to success. Trying to revitalize a downtown by cleaning up the decrepit buildings through diligent code enforcement, is only one part of a successful plan.

Code enforcement covers the "penalty" portion of the equation but does little to "revitalize". An excellent analogy would be the removal of drugs from a drug user. Although an important element in their rehabilitation, it will never be successful without providing an alternative that replaces the urge. As with the drug user, decaying downtowns need an alternative to further decay and that alternative is a robust "business focused" incentive program.

Because there are no competitive do-or-die pressures similar to what a business person operates under, it is extremely hard for cities to view downtown re-vitalization thorough the prism of a businessperson. Accordingly, most cities view incentives as give-aways with no clear return on investment.

In addition, the political ramifications can be daunting. On the surface, incentives can easily be made to look like special interests and corporate payoffs by political opponents during an election. It takes a strong politician, who is committed to re-development to stand up against those who would use those very incentives as a campaign issue. Even when a business has been "landed" and is doing well, it is extremely hard to show that the incentive was the difference maker. That is why so many towns "talk" re-vitalization, but don't have the will power to move forward on a comprehensive re-vitalization plan.

Unfortunately, you will never get business participation with more regulations. Because of their very nature, business abhors regulations. Anything that slows them down and prevents them from running their business, will be viewed instinctively as an unnecessary hindrance. That doesn't mean cities should relinquish all regulations It simply means that they use them along with a robust incentive program.

In addition, it's imperative that the city get the business community involved before exercising radical changes (e.g. polling existing proprietors about unsightly storefronts or dilapidated buildings). If the city makes the business community part of the solution, they will have a much greater chance of buy-in and resulting success.

Cities must think like a business owner. Not an easy task for those who have been in the public sector most of their lives. "If I was a business owner, what would it take to get me involved?"That should be the first question a city should ask. "If I'm struggling to make ends meet, what could I, my co-owners and the city do that would provide me with the best return on my investment".

The city must understand that since the city will still exist if an investment goes south but a business would quite possibly go out of business if that same plan fails, the level of scrutiny is much higher in the business world. When offering incentives, cities must not look at them as a city giveaway but instead should look at them as the business owner. The question should be, what is the level of risk for me, the business owner, versus the level of return for me. If the risk level, relative to the return, is too great, the plan will never move forward. Ask yourself, if I lost my job because the program was a failure, would I be so quick to engage?

In most cases, businesses will have to see some level of success (or some type of guarantee) before they will commit. Creating incentive programs alone will not do the trick. The city must be engaged. It must not only be an active participant but, especially at the onset, be the driver, with business buy in and participation at every step, to make it happen.

In addition, the city must publicize the progress that has had a direct effect on the business owners bottom line (present or future), not just the city's goals. No one wants to jump on board the titanic, even if it has the best deck lounge chairs. Everyone want's to be part of a winner. Cities should let all involved know, when they have a winner.

Unfortunately, that means that a city often has to initiate and fund the first moves, building a track record that can show quantifiable success. It doesn't always have to be in the bottom line. New benches, event signs, tree lined streets, street banners, downtown events all show that the city is alive and moving forward.

Renovation incentives, rent concessions to attract new businesses. Building facade incentives to "gussy up" existing businesses. All must be part of the mix.

Even the smallest success should be documented. Events, new facades, new business openings, new product mixes are newsworthy if presented in the proper vein. Get input from your local proprietors, talk to visitors and then send out a press release, using their quotes, to the local newspaper. Make sure your news articles are always written in the third person.

A discussion of why more business activity, equals more businesses, which in turn, equals more residents, that in the end, produces more papers sold, blogs read, etc. will help motivate your local newspaper, blogger, social networks, etc. to post all your press releases. The articles should speak about the success of the event (e.g. how many people attended, quotes from visitors and store owners, etc.). Your intent should be to create excitement. Show the success, through the eyes of existing and potential business owners. Every one of those articles should be part of your press kit and new business package.

If You Build It, They Will Come

Crumbzz International Bistro Pre-Build-Out

As with everything Crumbzz, once I knew we would be expanding our business model, a lot of thought went into what we would offer, where we would offer it, how we would present it and when we would begin.

The first issue was the name. We no longer were a bakery, but I surely didn't want to be a full blown restaurant. Bakeries are bright places with glass cases that display an assortment of baked items. Customers come in to purchase their baked goods and leave.

Restaurants, especially in America offer all kinds of foods in a multitude of environments but, their bottom line is usually focused on turning tables as quickly as possible and providing big, unhealthy offerings. Big and fast is their credo.

We were much more than a coffee shop and did not fit the definition of a cafe.

Our clients would come in to enjoy our offerings and enjoy each other's company. They would enjoy an atmosphere of style where old world brick meets stainless and marble.

After month's of discussions with my team, it was decided that the best name for what I was focused on achieving was a "Bistro".

My vision was pretty clear. As with our offerings, I view Crumbzz as much more than a product. I am totally focused on providing each one of our clients with an "experience".

From our website and blog, to our pre-sales support...our packaging and our offerings, through our post-sales client services...I wanted our bistro to not only compliment our mission but enhance it.

I was also focused on making sure our Crumbzz enthusiast gathering place was comfortable and welcoming. A place where Crumbzz enthusiasts could enjoy not only our offerings but, each others company in an environment that was warm and welcoming.

This brought to mind the wonderful European bistro's I had seen during my travels across Europe. These were places where one could come in, visit friends and family and stay as long as they liked. They would never be rushed in and out like the typical U.S. restaurant. Instead, as with all great European bistro's, they could sit as long as they liked, read the paper (or more likely today, read their tablet) and decompress.

Unlike U.S. restaurants, where the music is loud and upbeat (designed to "move em' in and move em' out quick), to encourage longer stays, the music at our bistro would be low and classic (Andrea Bocelli immediately came to mind).

Initially I called our location a European Bistro, but as my journey's expanded to Central America and South America, in search of the finest dishes to bring back to my bistro, I finally settled on International Bistro as the name that best fit our offerings.

Once I had our name secured, I moved on to the location. To serve our typical client, we were looking for an artsy, hip location. Initial forays in Dallas' included the typical artsy areas including: Deep Ellum, Bishop Arts, Uptown, Downtown, Cedars, etc. My team and I spent month's researching each area but in the end, found each missing one or more key ingredient.

The team then set our eye on the Dallas suburbs. Unfortunately, like most of the country, the suburbs in Dallas are chain focused. Because of our branding and price points, and our commitment to a socially active experience, we were definitely not a get em' in, get em' out chain focused business. And so, our search for the ideal location continued.

Building an international bistro was not initially in my plans. I had always seen the bistro as not only a place to sell my family's Crumbzz artisan crumb cakes but also as a social gathering place for Crumbzz enthusiasts.

Having done the "retail" thing before in New York, I was in no hurry to jump back into the grind once more. The hours, the pace, the challenges were all such a drag on my time and resources. But I felt it was important to have a place where we could meet our guests and get real-time, first-hand input on our offerings. That would all change when I received a call from Kim Buttram.

As the Executive Director for the City of Forney Economic Development Corporation (EDC). Kim had seen me on a recent TV program called *Good Morning Texas.* In my interview on that show, I was asked if Crumbzz was considering a retail location. Interestingly, the week before my appearance, I had been contacted by a suburban town called Sunnyvale who had inquired if we had an interest in locating a retail Crumbzz in their town. During that interview, I mentioned that we were scheduled to talk to a suburban town about just that.

Ten minutes after that interview, Kim contacted me and asked why Crumbzz had not considered Forney for its International Bistro.

Forney is a little town 23 miles east of downtown Dallas. Its claim to fame had been its once booming antique business corridor off highway 80. As interest in antiques began to wane, so too had Forney's downtown area. Led by Kim and the EDC, I soon learned that the entire town, from Mayor and City Council to the Building and Zoning Departments were all intent on reversing that trend.

How important is a forward thinking town? Can a town that has all participants on board to "listen" to our needs not only theirs actually change the dynamics of a business search?

Initially, I had no idea where Forney, Texas even was. In addition, I was only looking to investigate towns that bordered the Dallas metroplex. Forney, Texas was neither. It was a town, on paper, that I wouldn't have even considered. But, Kim made such a convincing argument of why a full blown bistro would benefit not only their town but also my company that it now became the leading contender for our first International Bistro.

As I mentioned in the previous chapter on what makes a vibrant downtown, they were willing to do whatever it took to make me successful but they needed my assurance that I would work with them to assure that success would benefit their town as well. After much soul searching, I acquiesced and committed to provide a place not only in a town not on my list of potential sites but also a bistro that was much more than simply a place to enjoy my family's cakes. This is what happens when you have a town that has a clear vision of who they are, where they want to be and understands what goals need to be accomplished not only for the town but also for the business owner. THIS is how you build a successful downtown!

Most towns are focused on attracting new businesses. Some even have a vision with grand plans in place. Unfortunately, few go any further than the design and planning stage and their plans lie dormant in their planning departments...great ideas, gathering dust.

At that time, under then Mayor Darren Rozell's guidance and City of Forney Economic Development Corporation Executive Director Kim Buttram's drive, Forney laid out a development plan that was different. It understood that a town must have an identity before it can move forward and that identity starts with the heart of any town, its downtown area.

A large part of their plan was focused on bringing life back to its downtown area. And the town wanted that life to be uniquely Forney. As Mayor Rozell explained. No one is going to go to Forney to eat at the Forney's Chili's. For downtown Forney, the Mayors vision was one of unique establishments that were only in Forney. The chains would be encouraged to locate on the two main roads that bisect the town of Forney, State Road 80 and Interstate 20.

The town was not interested in attracting chains and multi-site mega-stores to its downtown area. There are plenty of those in its outlying areas. Instead it was focused on encouraging small business' to set up shop to provide its residents and the multitude of visitors it hopes to attract, with a unique shopping experience.

Typical of most small Texas towns, Forney at that time had beautiful old buildings, sitting empty, just waiting to be brought back to life. This appealed to my focus on being green, and partnering with the local community. What better way to serve a local community than to resurrect an old existing building, help the town bring life back to its downtown area and partnering with local talent to make it all happen.

But vision is just part of the equation. Execution is even more important to assure success. And that's where Forney set themselves apart from all other towns.

Were there dissenters? You bet. Like most sleepy small towns, Forney had it's share of those who resented the towns growth and did everything possible to stop it but, as Herbert Hunt (one of our many gift cake clients) stated to me, "Fighting growth is like pushing against waves in the ocean. It will never stop, so you might as well plan for it."

Forney Mayor Rozell and Director Buttram were more than just focused on setting themselves apart, they were laser focused on placing Forney ahead of that growth.

Most restaurateurs would never consider placing their fine dining restaurant in a small sleepy town with such a small population. But, the more I thought about this sleepy town of Forney, instead of being concerned with its distance from the Dallas metro area with its large population of sophisticated diners, I saw this small town as a new and interesting challenge to my concept.

What would it be like to offer all those interesting international dishes that I brought back from across the world to small town America? Traditionally a meat and potatoes market, would they accept these dishes or would they only want home cookin'?

This is one of the many times when I would find myself at a crossroad that if I was willing to take a chance, would eventually lead me to where I am today. Call it karma, chance, good luck, opportunity, whatever, these are the path's that I believe are so important for one to take because they almost always lead to new and exciting successes.

It's All In The Details

Flags That Grace The Entrance To Forney Texas

In the previous chapter you learned that Forney, Texas was the city I chose to open my first International Bistro. That we chose Forney because they not only fit our mission of working with local providers, being as green as possible and assuring we were a responsible corporate citizen, but also because Forney seemed different, a town (excuse me, a CITY, as Buttram would always correct me) that had a clear vision of what it wanted to be and a leadership committed to fulfill that vision.

But, having a vision and the will to drive that vision are only part of the story. Because they are bureaucratic by nature, so many towns get bogged down in the details that end up killing the very vision they are promoting. Many a small business owner has watched in dismay as their hard work and plans have fallen to turf wars and ownership issues of small town governments. Deal killers arise along every step of the process. Government doesn't have to be big government to kill a small business. The tunnel vision of many small town departments clashes with the "how do we make it work" attitude of most small business owners. Planning and zoning departments that won't budge on zoning issues, building inspectors not interested in acceptable work-around's, by-the-book adherence to the "rules", are all issues that small business owners must overcome. My own experience working with other cities in the Dallas area provides an example of what small business owners must deal with.

As I mentioned previously, because of its size and population base, it was only logical that The City of Dallas was tops on our list for our first Crumbzz International Bistro. We looked at several areas. There were plenty of vacant buildings in areas we liked. Artsy areas like Deep Ellum, Bishop Arts, Uptown, Downtown, Cedar's, all had places that fit us nicely.

Most of the locations were empty buildings that were crying to be brought back to life. However, because we are a food establishment, the city required specific upgrades that drove our costs appreciably beyond our budget. These upgrades were hidden in the "bring the building up to code" requirement. You see in Dallas, if a building is vacant for more than six months it now has to be brought "up to code". Since most buildings in these areas have been empty for much longer than six months, a potential business would be saddled with costs that would never justify the projected income generation from the property.

Since the cost to "bring up to code" is so prohibitive, it often is cheaper to knock the building down and build new. But Dallas wants to "preserve" its heritage and won't let developers knock down its old buildings. And so, most of these great old buildings sit dormant on empty streets with little hope of a re-awakening.

I spoke to the Dallas EDC about this issue. Nice people, who understand the problem, but whose hands are tied because, as I were told by an EDC employee who asked not to be named, "right now the city is run by the planning and zoning department and they get their paychecks whether we have a vibrant community or a dead one." A sad, but all too common occurrence.

On the other end of the scale is Seagoville, the town we worked with before Forney "found" us. Seagoville's EDC is run by a committed Director who understands the need to breath life into the downtown area. Unlike Dallas' EDC, who has given in to the reality of their situation, Seagoville's EDC actively promotes their town and is aggressive in incentives and support to attract potential small businesses.

Unfortunately, the EDC of Seagoville goes it alone. Not because of an adversarial position with the rest of the towns departments. Ambivalent would be a better description of the rest of the town's view of its downtown area. Ambivalence can slow down the process but the main issue that prevents Seagoville from attracting businesses to its downtown area is the very property owners themselves. Resistant to change, unapproachable, unrealistic views of market conditions are key factors that prevent this little town from moving forward. And so Seagoville awaits a reality check of its owners and a commitment by its town before a re-awakening will occur.

And that's where Forney shined.

To successfully rehabilitate a downtown, you must have a department that champions the town's vision, an "owner" or "proponent" if you will. You'll find owners in many towns. Some are committed to the vision and drive relentlessly to make their vision come to life only to be stymied by the rest of the town's departments who see re-development as a challenge to their power bases. Other "owners" pay homage to the plan but little else, viewing the town's vision as a marketing tool rather than an actual re-development plan.

The proponent of Forney's vision was at the time Forney's Economic Development Corporation. The 7 member board, Director, Kim Buttram and her staff were relentless in their quest to turn Downtown Forney into a vibrant destination area. Kim and the EDC were one of the few fortunate champions who had a secret weapon to assure their success. That secret weapon was Mayor Rozell and a majority of the City Council.

Each proponent knew what needed to be done and where they could assist to make it happen. The vision of a new Downtown Forney was THEIR vision. Every department leader was briefed on the status of the plan and was proactive in how their department could help make the plan a success. How does that extrapolate down to the business owner? A few examples of our experience working with the City of Forney will serve to show how Forney was different.

Example #1: Bringing an old building "up to code" – Like Dallas, Forney wanted its buildings to be safe and up to code. Unlike Dallas, Forney offers the required tools for assistance for the business owner to make it happen. The EDC works directly with the involved departments on the who, what and where to complete the process. Financial incentive? Yes Forney provided a package that helped ease the pain, but it was the direct assistance that really made a difference.

Small business owners are focused on running their business and are often overwhelmed by the paperwork and process requirements of government. Director Buttram knew that Forney had an archaic permitting system, built to serve another time when only one or two businesses would apply. She personally facilitated the legwork to run those permits and inspections through to assure we met all those requirements. In short, the city made the cost financially acceptable AND the process seamless.

Example #2: Finding the right space – Forney helped us locate a wonderful old Victorian building on the outskirts of downtown, introduced us to the owner and helped package our offer. When that deal fell through, because the owner understandably did not want their kitchen expanded into a commercial kitchen, Forney found another building. When that space was found unsuitable for our use because of the lack of firewalls, the city made an unpredented decision. They actually traded their EDC offices with us so that we had a space suitable for our use! Tell me where you'll find that kind of commitment from any other city!

Example #3: City Involvement – Once we were open, Forney didn't drop the ball and hope revenues rolled in. Since the town viewed itself as our partner, they were with us all the way. Anything they could do to help make us more successful was open for discussion.

Grand Opening of Crumbzz Forney, Texas International Bistro

Our launch coincided with a full-page announcement in the local paper, a ribbon cutting black tie event for VIP's and a massive City of Forney grand opening ceremony for the general public. And Forney was a partner with us throughout the process, getting its officials out and the public involved each step of the way.

If you had to use one word to describe what set Forney above the rest, that word would be "Commitment", a commitment to making it happen. We found no other town to have it. We were proud to be the first in what would be the beginning of a string of many small business owners, who would help bring a "Uniquely Forney" downtown back to life. Our opening was simply the first step to awakening the downtown area. Now the hard work was to begin.

We knew that Crumbzz alone would not be enough to revitalize a downtown. The next step was to build a coalition of business owners that would actively promote the town. Make sure you had doers not joiners at its head. In Forney, the Chamber of Commerce was more focused on supporting and bringing businesses to all of Forney. In actuality, that extrapolated into placing companies in the easy areas like the main highways and highly visible zones. Downtown was definitely not on the Chambers radar. And so we created the Forney Downtown Business Association (FDBA). Members were focused solely on downtown Forney. The camaraderie that has been established between the city, the EDC and the FDBA has resulted in fantastic changes in the downtown area. In its first year, the FDBA successfully applied for and received hot funds to purchase street pole event banners, purchased and installed building outline lighting for the entire downtown area (a project that required the use of city and FDBA membership funds), and applied for TXDOT funds to line it's streets with trees, bushes and planters (a project that the city worked closely with the FDBA to assimilated into their downtown revitalization plan).

The success of the FDBA would not have happened without the direct assistance and nurturing by the city and the EDC. The city removed all obstacles and assisted in funding on many of our projects.

Understanding that the funds spent today would nurture the new organization and in the end, help move towards its goal of creating a vibrant downtown. The funding was viewed as an investment, not an expense. The EDC provided the focus and wherewithal to get the organization off the ground, it rallied existing members to actively participate, and it funded the FDBA's formation. All of this was necessary to assure the success of the effort.

The result, the downtown area now has several very publicized events. Local residents and visitors alike, visit the downtown area at night to see the building lights, our street lights and our event banner signs. All these small but important details provide a unique feel to historic downtown Forney. The city's master plan for our downtown has resulted in new roads, walkable sidewalks and more convenient parking.

That's all great but the real "SO WHAT" is that we have had several new businesses open, multiple existing businesses have used the facade incentive monies to red-do their buildings and signs, and the EDC is talking to an ever increasing number of potential new businesses who want to be "where the action is".

The bottom line here, is that the city must jump in with both feet (no toe dipping). It must show a commitment to spend the money, cut the regulations and lend a helping hand whenever and wherever it will make a difference. And, it must celebrate its victories by sharing them through a focused public relations program. Only then will you get full participation by the local business community. They may not wan't to jump on the titanic, but they also don't want to miss a boat that's ready to sail into a successful and vibrant downtown.

The Birth Of A Dream

It took over a year and a budget that grew with every added day, but the Crumbzz International Bistro became a reality on January 27, 2012. That's when Crumbzz held a black tie, invitation only party for the people who sacrificed their time and efforts to make our vision come to life.

Our 125 guests enjoyed fine food, great art and an insiders tour of our wonderful new facility.

On January 28th, we threw open our doors to the public with an official ribbon cutting and enjoyed the company of over 325 visitors who shared our cakes, coffee's and tea's as well as music by local musicians, flash mob poetry, pottery demonstrations, real-time art creations and more.

The following week we presented our complete menu, which included not only our cakes and Minizz snack cakes but also some rather unique offerings (more on those in a future chapter). But the star of all these events was clearly our new baby, our first International Bistro.

Located in Historic Downtown Forney, and built in the beautiful old Spellman Building, an 1880's structure that has sheltered many of Forney's finest, our International Bistro is truly a beauty to behold.

My father used to say that "everyone takes care of the big things, it is those who take care of the little things that make a difference" and we sure took care of the little things. Nothing was left to chance.

Fantiscritti Tuscany Italian Marble counters from the same quarry as Michelangelo's statue of David are complimented by Buckingham Slate floors and the original preserved bead wood ceiling.

Custom Corona accent lighting peeks through the beautifully sculpted, free-floating Velella sails that drift down from the ceiling. Authentic stage lighting is strategically placed to highlight the beautiful artwork of local artisans.

Sounds of Bocelli and Brightman fill the dining area, where guests enjoy the comfort of Carrera leather seating and sculptured aluminum tables, all designed to add to the chic feel of this exquisitely contemporary pavilion.

Each element is designed to provide our guests with an environment where they feel comfortable to kick back and enjoy the moment.

The unique look and feel of the International Bistro has already attracted attention from architects (famed architectural photographer Howard Doughty was one of our first visitors to photograph the many unique architectural elements of our pavilion) to movie producers (the producers of the short film New Hope found Crumbzz the perfect location to set the stage for their film, which was aired at the LA 168 film festival).

Most importantly, our new home has gotten rave reviews from our guests.

To accomplish something as intricate as this project proved to be, I needed experts in each area that knew how to overcome the challenges we encountered on a daily basis.

I had a very specific vision of what our International Bistro should look like and how it should function. Choosing the right architect and general contractor were key elements in bringing that vision to reality.

After month's of research, the design work was awarded to Ron Hobbs Architects out of Garland, Texas and the construction of the project to General Contractor, Craig Randall Custom Remodeling from Forney, Texas.

Ron and his team were instrumental in converting our vision into reality. Their creative process enabled us to bring oftentimes vague ideas into fruition.

Praising the work of Ron and his team would not be complete without mentioning Wadona Stich, Ron's Director of Interior Design. Wadona's vision and focus on making this a memorable project, on all levels, was absolutely amazing. It became evident early on that the beauty of the design and quality of materials would not have happened without her direct involvement in every facet of the project.

Laying out on paper what needs to be done and how it should be completed is worth little if the general contractor, the person who oversee's the actual construction of the project, is lacking in talent, commitment or ability.

Craig Randall had plenty of each. Craig's intent to create nothing short of a masterpiece was evident in every facet of the job. Craig made sure the project reflected our vision and our architects requirements. He often went the extra mile in suggesting "improvements" whenever he noted an area that he felt could be improved, savings in areas that could be economized and workarounds for areas that could not be built as designed.

There were so many craftsman that were instrumental in the project coming together as envisioned and we are unable to name them all here, but a few stand out because of their amazing commitment to excellence.

Craftsman Jose Rodriguez of Natural Stone Designs who hand selected and crafted our beautiful marble counters into functioning works of art; Austin Home Restorations out of Orlando, Florida, who installed one of the most stunning slate floors you will ever find in a bistro and did it over a challenging (half cement, half wood base structure), in the middle of our busiest construction days;

Intex Electric, who proved that they were more than capable of solving the multiple lighting requirements of an art gallery, guest dining and culinary creation center that required multiple types of energy efficient spot lighting throughout;

Sun Painting who precisely matched our multiple color schemes and finishes and was also able to the create the intricacies of achieving a multi-dimensional metallic finish in our culinary development area that met not only our extreme design requirements but also the county health department commercial kitchen requirements.

Our list would not be complete without including the committed members of The Forney Arts Council who planned, developed and hung the beautiful art work throughout the pavilion and finally The City of Forney whose dedication to create a special place in their historic downtown was evident throughout the project.

A Bistro Unlike Any Other

The Crumbzz International Bistro

Experience...Experience...Experience

These three words ring constantly through my head when you talk about dining out. To me providing a great meal is just a great meal if the ambiance, service, even the music is not special.

To receive a special night out, you have to take care of EVERYTHING. There can be no lapses in any area. This was the prime thought that resonated with me when I started the challenge of building my bistro.

As with my cakes, where the packaging was just as important as the offering inside, my bistro had to be the complete package or I wasn't interested in doing it.

There are tons of places that offer the "best this or that". I wanted to offer not only the best but something entirely unique. My bistro would be the tool to get me to that place.

The design had been floating around in my head for years, one of those..."If I did this, it would have to offer that" kind of things. We would stand out by offering unique breakfast and lunch/brunch dishes from around the world, crafted by classically trained chef's in a completely different environment.

Breakfast and lunch restaurants are not unique in the USA by any stretch of the imagination. Every city has hundreds of them. Even every small town has a diner that serves breakfast and lunch. BUT, breakfast and lunch dishes from around the world, crafted by classically trained chefs in a fine dining atmosphere, served by well trained servers is!

Classically trained chefs are usually only found in fine dining restaurants that offer dinner. Their training is usually focused exclusively on that very thing. Unique dishes? You'll only find those for dinner as well. NO ONE is ever focused on a unique way to make oatmeal or eggs!

In the U.S., everything is about speed. Get em' in, get em' out. Drive throughs, fast food and big (cheap) offerings. I thought there was a place for something different and I was about to find out if I was right or wrong.

During my travels around the world, I grew fond of the European style of dining and the unique twists European chefs took to craft outstanding dishes. Each visit was more an experience than a meal and I decided this would be the special experience our bistro would offer in America.

Accordingly, my bistro was designed and built to have a uniquely European bistro feel, where art, music & our culinary creations coexisted in harmonious symphony. I wanted the offerings and atmosphere to be more like Italy or France than small town Texas.

I made sure my family's 400-year old Austrian recipe Crumbzz artisan crumb cakes would always be represented there. The music I would choose would not be your typical "metro" music with its thump, thump beat, played loudly throughout the restaurant. This type of music is played in most U.S. restaurants to encourage guests to order fast, eat fast and leave.

The music we would play would be low (to allow one to hear each other talk) and feature the sounds of Bocelli & Brightman. This would encourage guests to slow down and enjoy each others company. To further our guest's "experience", we would seat them on Carrera leather seating surrounding sculpted aluminum tables which, is a true bistro style look. Our Italian marble counters, and the Smoky Mountain blue slate floors would add to the chic feel of our contemporary dining pavilion. The contrast between our old building and our chic modern interior would be breathtaking.

As an added feature, I wanted to surround our open kitchen with a bistro bar to allow guests to view our classically trained chef's at work. This area would be a favorite area for foodies who love to cook. Our bistro bar would provide them with a direct view of how great dishes are crafted by dedicated chefs.

The beauty of my bistro would be the perfect setting for my international menu. Many of the dishes I had already found during my travels. We would feature those in a limited offering. To be great one has to do what one does best. I did not want to be another Denny's® with a giant menu of every dish known to mankind. I would rather offer a limited menu of dishes, crafted to perfection versus ton's of dishes done mediocre at best.

I decided that we would offer a limited amount of dishes with different specials only during the holidays. The initial dishes I chose to offer would include; Gaufre Liège waffles from Austria; Gamberaia blueberry ricotta pancakes, Caprese salad, Roma tomato basil soup from Italy; Gruyere egg soufflés, two types of Parisienne quiche, a classic French Onion Soup Gratinée and bruléed oatmeal from France; Fribourg grilled cheese from

Germany; Albacore tuna salad's and sandwiches from Denmark; Nochalette's from Mexico and although it would be an international bistro, I had to add my favorite breakfast dish from my hometown New York City (to Texans, New York City is a foreign country anyway), Taylor Ham & eggs on a Kaiser roll.

Each of these international offerings would be made exactly as they were made in their respective countries. Today, as my travels continue, I add new dishes but keep our offerings limited to no more than thirty dishes at any one time.

I've often heard how great it is to pursue your passion, etc – but I've spoken with enough people to know that it's a lot harder to do than to say.

As with my cakes, at my bistro, I wanted to create an "experience" not just a great dish. With that in mind, every detail was considered. Our tableware is weighted and not the standard cheap version found in most restaurants. Our salt and pepper shakers come from the Museum of Natural art, our bistro is color coordinated from the ovens, refrigerators, cutting boards to the napkins. The art on our walls is from local artists and is changed every two months, our patio dining area is tree lined and mulch covered to allow pets free roam. Nothing about my bistro is plain vanilla.

Unlike American restaurants, which are all about large quantities of cheap food, served quickly to get 'em in and get 'em out, everything about my bistro is designed to provide a pleasant socially conducive dining experience. My favorite comment from our dining guests is one that is heard quite often "we actually decompressed from our busy day and just enjoyed the company and the meal."

Healthy Eating Never Takes A Back Seat

I have always been focused on healthy eating and was one of the first restaurants not to accept milk with chemical additives. Today, all my offerings are previewed by a nutritionist to assure we are maximizing our potential to provide healthy, chemical free dishes. My nutritionist has been extremely helpful in making as she states, "the most healthy pancakes you'll ever have". She explained why we need to buy our milk from Jersey or Guernsey cows only (you'll learn why in another chapter), what the difference is between Celiac disease and gluten intolerance and how we can serve clients that suffer from either one and she taught me and my staff just WHAT goes into healthy eating.

At my bistro, we take healthy eating seriously and take it into account with each and every dish.

It's Not For Everyone

I am resolute that we make all our dishes from scratch using the finest ingredients. That sounds great but it does have a downside that is simply not acceptable to many Americans. You see, unlike the rest of the world, where dining is predominantly all natural and a social engagement that can last for hours, America is home to the drive in window, the get em' in get em' out fast land of big dishes.

Since my bistro uses only the finest ingredients we are not a discount chain that piles the food high and sells it fast and cheap. The every day American does not understand that a restaurant has to make a profit, and in order to make a profit, the bigger the dish, the cheaper the ingredients. This is a yin/yang fact that is simply irrefutable.

I do not care to make any dish or cake fast and cheap. Since we make EVERYTHING from scratch, we are not the place to eat if you're in a hurry. We get reviews all the time. Most of them are great, touching on the great food and service. If we ever get a bad review it's usually because the reviewer feels we are too slow. I couldn't agree with them more.

Great food takes time to make and great food that is made to order takes even more time. If you don't have the time to wait and enjoy your food, we are not the place for you.

It's All In The Experience

When I first envisioned offering the family Crumbzz artisan crumb cake to the rest of the world, I wanted the offer to befit this wonderful part of my family's history.

My family always knew we had something special. And the lines of Cakers at our New York bakery, anxiously awaiting the next cake to arrive, hot out of the oven, only confirmed that others also felt our cake was something special.

Understanding how special our offer was, I knew that Crumbzz had to be much more than simply an artisan cake purveyor or restaurant. Our offer had to be an experience —an experience that our clients and guests would always remember.

Building an experience is in many cases much harder than you might imagine. Making my cake and opening my bistro was all about the big thing. Building an experience was all about the little things.

THE DIFFERENCE ONE WORD CAN MAKE - You may have noticed that I never use the word customer. I choose the word "client" for my online sales and "guest" for my bistro visitors because it goes to the heart of the relationship my staff and I have with each person who chooses to enjoy our offerings and company.

The dictionary states that a customer is "a person or organization that buys goods or services from a store or business." Customer infers a one-time thing, a single act of making a purchase. There is no mention of a relationship.

A client on the other hand is all about an ongoing relationship, as in an attorneys relationship with their client.

At my bistro, we don't have customers. We have guests. To me, it's all about the relationship. If we make a onetime sale, we have failed. It's not about sales it's about building a relationship with our client and creating an experience for our guests that lasts years.

Although the client and guest is our primary focus, our relationships go much deeper. At Crumbzz, the relationships we have with our employees, our vendors, our farmers and even the chicken who lays our eggs, are all important.

THE CLIENT/GUEST DYNAMIC - After the quality of the offering, our client's/guest's experience is most influenced by how we interact with each and every one. How we assist each of our clients:
- on the phone;
- how well our website and smartphone app's are focused on their needs;
- the attention we pay when they walk in the door of our bistro;
- how interesting our Twitter and Facebook posts are;
- how well we make our dishes;
- how attentive we are to their needs,

are all important touch points.

I have spent month's working through each and every one of these areas to make sure I haven't missed a thing.

I have developed each area to service a different need. Our website is designed to provide information on our company, our product and our mission. It allows clients to place their order with confidence they will arrive on time, freshly baked from the oven. Our gift cards and chef signed "Perfection" cards are designed to provide a personal touch not found in todays commercial mass-produced world.

With its beautiful design, comfortable seating, soft music and unique international offerings, our bistro is designed to provide our guests with a refuge from the days stress. A place were friends and family can meet to enjoy each other company.

Our social media Twitter, Facebook and Instagram presence provide quick updates on Crumbzz happenings a new offering or a new event we are sponsoring. It is also the place where Crumbzz enthusiasts can talk to each other and to us.

My blog and my books are where I am able to provide my clients and guests with a deeper understanding of who we are, what we do and how we get there. I want my books to be a place where you grab a cup of coffee and a slice of your favorite Crumbzz cake and take a leisurely stroll through the world we call Crumbzz. Learn a little, laugh a little and simply enjoy the experience.

When you call us on the phone you will get a real person. You won't be asked to press 1 to go to a recording and then 2 to go to the next recording.

If you email us you will get an answer within 24-hours. And your answer will be from a real person.

In most cases, your Crumbzz cake or Minizz snack cakes will arrive within 2-4 days of your order. They will be hand made to order for every request, and accordingly, will always be fresh, without the use of any chemical preservatives.

Your meal at our bistro will be unlike any you have ever had, from countries across the world, prepared from scratch by classically trained chefs. It will be served with fine silverware, custom cups that maximize the aroma of your coffee or tea and placed on classic bistro table by committed servers who are intent on making your visit memorable.

One thing our clients and guests can be sure of, is that we look at everything. Nothing is taken for granted because what we are building is a relationship and relationships take time to build but are always everlasting.

We're Having A Party

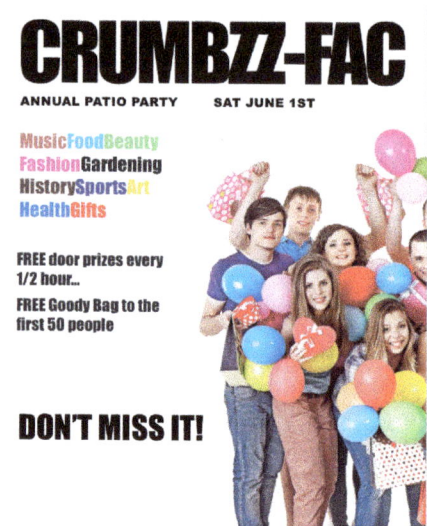

Every year, Crumbzz celebrates the start of the spring-summer season at our Forney International Bistro with a patio party. We usually hold it late May to early June. It sounds pretty mundane and straight forward. Announce the party to your local clientele, put together a few fun things to do, pretty up the patio and zippo, your ready to go. NOT! I can tell you from our experience with each party, it's not close to simple.

Now I realize that part of the problem may be me. As a perfectionist, I have my hands in everything and what starts out as a simple project often balloons into a major event. Be that as it may, I thought you'd like to know just what goes into an event such as this and so here's a brief rundown of our first patio party.

PLANNING

My staff and I started planning for this event in February. In February, we sat down and white boarded what we thought should go into the event. What can we handle and what is over and above our capabilities.

We then met with our partners, to discuss event ideas, logistics and the division of responsibilities. From that point on, we met weekly until the day of the event to update our progress, discuss challenges and fill any holes. Since we let the Forney Art Council (FAC) use our walls as their art gallery, we partnered with the the FAC for the event. Our contact at the FAC was Liz Lawless. Liz had experience in marketing, radio, as well as the art world and she proved to be invaluable in assisting us in creating a successful event.

There were several given's; Live music, a new product release, art demonstrations, prizes and gifts, were among the chosen highlights decided upon by the team. Other ideas (like the involvement of other town vendors, a before and after makeover, etc., came through the creative process. In the end, we felt that we had a pretty good package that would provide something for everyone.

PRODUCT DEVELOPMENT

We thought that the patio party would prove to be an ideal vehicle to introduce a new flavor of our artisan crumb cake. Since it was the beginning of summer, I wanted the new flavor to be something that would speak to summer. From concept to product development to tastings and back again to development, time and time again, creating a new flavor is a timely process that can take several months.

This particular development curve took a little over four months. We tried a multitude of flavors on our more than willing local guests. Some were okay, others we just couldn't get to where we wanted them to be, no matter how many attempts.

Finally after eliminating the also rans, we came down to five contenders; Baileys® Irish Cream, Key Lime Pie, Red Velvet Cake, Strawberry Cheesecake and Strawberry Rhubarb. In the end, the Key Lime Pie won the day. It definitely spoke to summer, and the tart lime complimented our sweet Crumbzz artisan crumb cakes beautifully.

(Although the Key Lime Pie was the winner, we liked the Strawberry Rhubarb so much that we introduced it in June for a short one month offering that turned out to be quite popular.)

Although our cake tasting took time, what we didn't realize is that developing a new flavor cake would be the easiest part of the whole event!

TOWN INVOLVEMENT

Since Forney's Historic Downtown was starting to experience a re-birth, we thought it would be best to make our first patio party not only OUR patio party but to use it as a "meet and greet" event for ALL downtown vendors.

Putting together multiple vendors is a bit like herding cats. And our cat's were everywhere. We wanted to have a steady flow of activities throughout the day. Music, art, fashion, were all part of the equation.

Putting together all the different events and choreographing them to seamlessly work together was no simple task.

We asked a local women's boutique named Groovy's to join us and provide a fashion show of their clothing. Most small town vendors are not marketing savvy. Explaining the how, what and where can be a real challenge. Groovy's owner, Christi Foster, was one of the few vendors who was marketing savvy. She came up with a different twist using well known local woman as models.

We also included for the first time another local ladies fashion boutique, Plush, to show off their designs.

Not sure why but, getting local musicians to perform during the day proved to be much harder than imagined. The FAC, handled the musicians. Thank God, because up to the day of the event, they were still scrambling to pin down acts.

We came up with what we thought was a catchy idea to have one of our local beauty salons (Touch Up Beauty) choose a willing participant to subject themselves to a "Before" & "After" makeover, complete with photographs and all. That idea turned out to be a big hit.

Since the Forney Historical Society has a beautiful museum right down the block from us, we got them to speak about Forney history and to show some never before seen photos of our town.

The FAC corralled two artists (Michael Gillespie & Kathy Mackey) to paint live in front of our International Bistro and a Spinner (Susan Holden) to provide an interesting historic spinner demonstration.

The FAC also agreed to hold their Festival Poster Design Contest during the patio party with local celebrity judges handling the gala event.

To wrap up the day, local horticulturist John Homesley of Homesley Landscaping & Gardening spoke about summer gardening tips on our patio.

GOODY BAG COUPONS/CERTIFICATES

Getting a multitude of participants was just one side of the party. We also asked every vendor in the downtown area to donate coupons/ certificates, etc. We used these gifts to fill a goody bag, which we gave out to the first 50 guests. Getting coupons/certificates, etc. proved to be one of our biggest challenges. Although we ended up representing most of the local vendors, most had never printed a coupon/certificate, which forced us to improvise with business cards as promo's for the offerings we created.

The goody bag certificates and coupons turned out to be a great success but needed much more advance planning and time budgeted than we expected.

DOOR PRIZES

To add to the excitement, we put together eleven special door prizes to be presented every half hour to a lucky guest. From dinner for two, wine glasses, plants, paintings, antiques, music and designer tote bags, there was something for everyone. Since we didn't want people sitting at a table all day waiting to see if they won a gift, we made it so entrants did not have to be there for their winnings. We had each entrant fill out a card with their name, email address, and phone number. Although we were tasked with having to contact every winner by email/phone, we felt this was a better method and would be welcomed by all participants.

This program was actually easier than we thought, as most vendors had something that they could provide that would ideally represent their professions.

ADVERTISING

One of the biggest challenges was how to advertise our party. With no budget to speak of, advertising became a real challenge. No one reads the newspapers any more so a donated ad in the paper would get, at best, limited exposure. The FAC did manage to get our event in a couple of magazine "calendar of events" sections.

Crumbzz and the FAC also sent an email blast to all our clients and members and Facebook, Twitter and Instagram were valuable arrows in our quiver. *(BTW, we use MailChimp to create and distribute all our email blasts. They work great for us and best of all, they are free).*

Finally, we asked our participating vendors to let their customers know about the event by posting promo's at their point of sale.

MEASURING SUCCESS

Our formula for rating the success of our patio party consisted of four elements.
- Did it bring people downtown?... Check ✓
- Did it introduce people to the many vendors we have in

    our growing downtown?.... Check✓
- Did it generate business and exposure for us & the FAC?... Check ✓
- Did it generate business for our partnering vendors?...
    TBD?

Hard to tell how successful it was. Since most of the participating vendors had no real method to track. For any future events a tracking method would need to be incorporated so we would know the real value to all participating vendors.

Hello, Let Me Introduce Myself

One of the key ingredients of our success has nothing to do with flour, sugar, butter or cinnamon. Nor does it have anything to do with our beautiful packaging or our passionate approach to serving our clients and guests. It does however, have everything to do with marketing.

Nowadays there are so many ways to get the word out, choosing what form of media to use often seems overwhelming. To add to the confusion, most entrepreneurs are understandably, so focused on the care and development of their product that marketing is usually a second thought. Since marketing is often out of their comfort zone it often ends up playing second fiddle to everything else. It Shouldn't!!

Most entrepreneurs mistake marketing for advertising. They don't understand that telling the world about their product is just one aspect of marketing. Marketing does include advertising, but for a new business especially, it also includes positioning or branding. An existing business that has established its position in the market, can focus primarily on advertising their product. A new business must first tell their target market who they are, what they stand for and most importantly, what their clients can expect of them. In short they must define their position in the world.

From the beginning, I knew we had the finest Crumbzz artisan crumb cakes in the world and with the opening of our international bistro in 2012, the most unique international offerings for breakfast, brunch and lunch this side of the pond but, I also understood that no one else knew that. I also knew, what we stood for, who we were, and to me, what we stood for was inescapably joined with our offerings.

When it comes to marketing, most small businesses tend to think small. Advertising in the local newspaper, coffee table TV guide, door-to-door hand-outs posting on Facebook, Twitter and Instagram but, nothing more. However, the "norm" is exactly what you don't want to do if you want to be successful. If you want to grow big, you need to think big.

I wanted our offerings to make a difference, not only for our clients and guests but also for those who work for us and those who work so hard on the farm, ranch and plantation. I wanted to have an effect on not only our own carbon footprint but also on how others affect the world we live in. If we were going to do our small part to change the world, we had to grow big enough to make a difference. With that in mind, I took a different, non-traditional route. I chose to do NO advertising. Although, not the norm, I have always believed that it's better to have a happy client or guest tell someone about us than to have us tell someone about us. Don't get me wrong, we may not have advertised in the traditional sense, but we did get the word out. I just used another form to get to our target market and that form of advertising is called Public Relations.

Wikipedia defines Public Relations (PR) as *"the practice of managing the spread of information between an individual or an organization (such as a business, government agency, or a nonprofit organization) and the public."*

PR is ideal for painting a picture about your company and it's products. In most cases, if done properly, it has the credibility of having someone else talk about you. But, in order to have an effective PR program, you must have a story to tell. If your story is newsworthy, it will be picked up by the media, grassroots organizations and individuals and be told over and over.

Most companies operate under the premise that a "better" product or "cheaper" price are the best motivators to get potential clients to follow them. My belief is that, because it is used so frequently (doesn't everyone say they have a "better" widget), following this path results in a "so what" consumer reaction.

Because I will never cheapen the quality of our offerings, to sell at a "cheaper" price than the competition, this strategy was not an option for me. In addition, PR on price or quality is old school and almost never newsworthy. It's my belief that in order to create an effective PR program, you must have a story that the media wants to tell because the public will find it interesting enough to read.

There are stories in most every company. You just need to know where to find them. I was fortunate to have the history of my family's four-hundred year old family Crumbzz artisan crumb cake recipe as the foundation for the "Crumbzz Story". But I didn't stop there. Because I traveled across the world for the finest ingredients, I knew THAT would also make an interesting story.

If you follow Crumbzz, you know we are very green minded. Three percent of our profits go into our non-profit Crumbzz Green Foundation and we actively promote sustainable farming, fair trade and eco-friendly operations. All of those points are story lines, in and of themselves. In addition, we continue to be interviewed on the unique dishes we offer at our first international bistro. Why? Because in choosing a small town with little or no discernible business activity, we helped bring life back to their historic downtown area. We made sure there was a storyline on bringing dishes from across the globe to small town America.

I don't just wait for the media to find us. I continually send out press releases on anything I think will be of interest to readers, including, new product offerings, our patio parties, the stories behind new restaurants and specialty stores that carry our cakes, to list just a few.

I have even made an event out of the addition of a giant rain barrel to water our plants. If you think hard enough, you can find the story out of most anything.

TWO CAVEATS:

ONE: We never try to sell anything in a PR piece. We do however, believe that everything, if positioned correctly, is newsworthy. For it to be successful, it **MUST** be newsworthy. We look at every PR piece and ask ourselves, would someone find this interesting? Would they like to read this?

TWO: Writers and reporters are human. Being human, they tend to like well written pieces that leave them with little or no editing to do. If they have to spend the time re-writing a piece, it better be one heck of a story or it will never see the light of day. Short and to the point pieces are are the best, with a "hook" headline (a headline that will draw them to read further).

For those of you with small businesses who are thinking of starting your own PR campaign, make sure that if you can't write, you have someone who can, write your PR pieces. Oh, and don't get upset if they make changes to your masterpiece. Their main goal is often different than yours and may not match up with your grand vision. Who do we send our press releases to? Most people would think we send to media outlets that focus on food and dining. Not so. Yes we send to those organizations, but we also send to downtown development magazines, environmental media, travel sites and city life magazines, as well as bloggers that cover multiple spectrums, to name just a few.

As we mentioned above, you'll also notice that every PR piece we send out is true to our branding or company/product position. This helps us build on who we are and what we stand for and helps our client or guest know who they are dealing with.

Today, traditional media is no longer the only way to reach potential clients and guests. In fact some of the newer forms of social media are as important or in some cases, more important than traditional marketing mediums. Understanding our client base and targeted market led us directly to these forms of client interaction. Why? Because that is where our clients are.

Building a Website...The Long Winding Road To Nowhere

It hasn't been easy, but we finally got there on February 6, 2011, the Crumbzz website was finally launched...kind of! It took twelve month's and three website developers to get there, but we finally made it...sort of!

My long and painful journey actually started in February 2010 when I sat down and sketched out my ideas for the site. By March, I had a basic idea of what I wanted. Elegant, clean, little or no advertising, less is more, was the basic theme.

The nature of our offerings dictated my market focus to a client who is socially and environmentally conscious and appreciates the finer things in life.

Accordingly, my site had to be upscale with beautiful pictures of our offerings. I also wanted the landing page to feature a stylish flash type feature that was of visual interest yet simple and understated.

From a technical standpoint, because my intent was to be equally accessible from a desktop, laptop, as well as tablets and smartphones, I wanted the site built in a computer language that all could see. And that language I was told was html5.

For those of you who are technically challenged like me, html5 is a computer language that allows flash type elements (in its simplest terms, elements that move) to be viewed on smartphone's and tablets.

Prior, when you saw these types of elements, they were usually created in Adobe Flash. However, Flash at the time of our build was slowly being phased out.

Since I believe that accessing a website on an smartphone or tablet is how most of our clients and guests will gain access to us and the fact that my target client relies on these devices today, I wanted to be where the action was.

However, building a site in html5 posed a problem. When they first built my site back in 2011, html5 was a relatively new computer language, and there was not a lot of "off the shelf" modules to choose from.

Most websites were built using pre-built modules that are slightly customized for their particular site. This saves time and money (time is money when building a site).

Since the module has been used extensively in the real world, not only do you save time on the build but you also save time on the testing.

Because the developers were using html5, they had to write and test all their code to assure it worked as intended. This is no easy task.

In addition, the Crumbzz site was pretty complicated. With multiple levels of ordering (we market to retail clients, exclusive specialty stores and high-end restaurants) and multiple offerings that include our

Crumbzz Cakes, Minizz snack cakes and fashion items. To add on top of this, we also allow clients to send different gift messages with each cake. Accordingly, the site was a real challenge to build.

With all this going on, my first developer got the site up to the testing phase before they crashed (went out of business). Four month's of development and my 50% up front money went with them.

Using the code created from my first developer, my second developer set about to complete the site. Three month's into the project, I was informed that they were unable to build the voting area of the site to the required spec's and would have to start from scratch to make it work.

My third developer, a highly recommended developer from New York, assured me that he would be able to accomplish what seemed like the impossible dream.

When I received the "finished product" I received a site that had no back-end access to allow my webmaster to update items and adjust offerings and meets few of my requirements for our client's needs. I wanted a site that enables clients to...

- Check out the story of Crumbzz, look into our heart and soul and read about what goes into each of our offerings... CHECK✓
- Cruise through our client's own words and be able to reserve multiple cakes sent to multiple addresses... NOPE X
- Scale from desktop to tablet to smartphone... NOPE X
- Check out our gifting programs or visit "Fashionably Crumbzz" to see our latest fashions... CHECK✓
- Enter a recipe, vote on recipe idea or find all our contact information... NOPE X

- Have an administrative back-end that is simple to use to update the site.... NOPE X

If you view our site as of today, you'll notice that our site does not scale to smartphones or tablets, does not allow you to place multiple cake orders with multiple gift cards to be shipped to multiple addresses and although you can't see it, still has no back-end administrative area for us to make changes.

To be quite honest, this was a team project and my whole team was exhausted from the whole process and I have, ever since, (since we have already paid three different developers up front monies, with no visible achievement) been reluctant to pay the normal asking price of 50% up front and the balance upon completion, to the NEXT developer who will "assure us" that they can get it right.

We have applied several band aid fixes to make our site usable (but not scalable) but, to date, we are nowhere near the vision I had. It is one of the few things that I have been unable to make a success and it remains a constant thorn in my side.

From your desktop and to a lesser extent your tablet (forget about your smartphone), our site will show you beautiful pictures of our cake and bistro offerings and although not intuitive, you can place single orders for our cakes and view every dish available at our bistro. In addition, you can also view our bistro menu and party planner. BUT, if you care to order multiple cake orders we suggest customers call us and actually have stated that fact with our number on our website.

Hopefully, you'll find using it, easier than we did building it. Keep in touch, who knows, we may someday find a solution to this ongoing, never-ending saga.

How We Use Social Networks

I'm always amazed at how businesses use social media. In most cases there seems to be two schools of thought. Either its a necessary evil that "I'll put stuff on, so I can say I'm there" or what a great advertising vehicle, "I'll advertise my ass off to generate business!" In both cases, the business owner is going to end up feeling that social media is much ado about nothing!"

In each case, the business owner has completely missed what social media is all about. The power of social media is hidden in broad daylight in its very name. "SOCIAL MEDIA" is all about a "media" for "social" interaction. Facebook, Twitter, LinkedIn, Pinterest, Instagram, YouTube and to a lesser degree, Yelp, Trip Advisor and Google + and the like, all provide platforms for users to interact, share and express common interests.

A business owner who discourages or worse, prevents input or "posts" from users, is not using the power of the network and in many cases is telling users that the business is NOT socially connected or worse, adversarial to their networked users.

Owners who view their social network presence as a great place to advertise, are also missing the boat. Social interaction is all about providing users with something they want to read. Something they will find interesting. Something that they will want to share with others. Very few advertisements fall into this category.

Although we are not the most cutting edge company to use social networks, we are active and have found that they are a useful tool to keep in touch with our clientele, to get client feedback and yes...to generate business.

At Crumbzz, we use several social media outlets. Besides our web page and blog, you can find us on Facebook, Twitter, Pinterest, Yelp, Trip Advisor, Google + and YouTube. Each provides a different outlet and allows us to generate a different message.

I look at our website as a place where we build our brand and image and where clients can place orders. If a client wants to know about our products, get an overview on who we are or place an order, our website is the place to go.

My blog is designed to provide a drill down or "deep dive" into the heart and soul of our company. In-depth articles provide readers with an unusually thorough view of who we are and what we do. It is where I am truly able to build and present my brand. If a client wants to really get to know what makes us tick, they will will get it all on my blog.

On Facebook I provide a weekly video I'll read one of the chapters of one of my books and a weekly "kitchen tip" from my first "Quest For The Best" book. I sprinkle in news events, monthly new offerings, and bistro party events. When we want to join in with fellow enthusiasts and actually have a real ongoing relationship, Facebook is where I make that happen.

If our blog is a "deep dive", Twitter is for shallow waters. It's for my short, off-the-cuff comments on things I think our followers will find interesting. Quick thoughts, witty musings, help me build our brand and reinforce our corporate personality.

One of the things I am intently focused on is our presentation. From cakes to bistro dishes, I am intent on providing our enthusiasts with a complete experience. What better place to do that than on Pinterest. I must confess that my bistro guests are the ones who got us on Pinterest by taking pictures of our dishes at our International bistro. I now make sure we have photos of every dish we create, every cake we offer, for all to view. For all those "visual" potential guests who need to **see it first**, Pinterest is where I give them a great look at our many creations.

I am always being interviewed by the media about our history, worldwide searches for the finest ingredients, environmental causes, historic downtown activities, personality seminars, etc. YouTube is my favorite place to provide followers with access to all those video's. I also like to use YouTube to play video's that further causes I believe in, such as environmental, fair trade and natural ingredients. It doesn't have to be about Crumbzz to get on my YouTube site. YouTube is another outlet to build on our brand and let our followers and enthusiasts know what other people think of us and what we stand for.

You may have thought it odd that I also included Yelp, Trip Advisor and Google + to the list of social networks. You can add to that list Urban Spoon, Local Eats, Open Table and Food Spotting. Although I don't post to these sites, per se, I do make sure we are listed, photos and all, for all to see. I know…we've heard from many restauranteurs that they have a love/hate affair with these types of services because, as one of my chef friends stated, "It's only a matter of time before you piss someone off and they're always the one's that post. The one's that love you never post." That may be true in some cases, but I find that if you really take care of your guests they'll take care of you and let the world know.

Yes we'll get an occasional post (usually about why we don't have cokes, sweet and low, etc. (because they are chemicals or have chemicals in them) or that we are not speedy like Waffle House (because we make everything from scratch) but in most cases, we get wonderful reviews that assure us that we are taking care of our family of enthusiasts. If you want them to find you, you **MUST** be on these sites. There isn't a day that goes by that we don't meet and greet a new guest from one of these sites. If you're comfortable enough with your offerings and service to let others speak about your offerings, these sites are the place to be.

You'll notice, that I did not mention advertising on any of these sites. Yes my website is created to sell cakes and bistro offerings but even there, I provide a place to make your order but never try to oversell the product. Instead we describe what and how we create and let the visitors imagination carry them to the ordering page.

Why no advertising? Because it is my belief that you should never blatantly advertise on social media sites. Yes, on Facebook, we talk about our cake of the month (we create an unusual flavor each month and make it available for only that month) and we do talk about upcoming events, but we do this in an informational format, NEVER as an advertisement. On YouTube we are content to let others talk about us.

I have found (and hundreds of studies have shown) that the quickest way to turn off (and quickly lose) a visitor on social media, is to advertise to them.

So why be involved in social media if it doesn't generate $$$$$? Simple. First of all, it does generate $$$$, just not in the traditional sense. As mentioned sites such as Yelp, Trip Advisor, Google +, Urban Spoon, Local

Eats, Open Table and Food Spotting generate business for us every day.

Although we can't always see it, people who read posts on Facebook, Twitter, see pictures on Pinterest and videos on YouTube, get to know us and reach a comfort level that allows them to try what we have to offer. Can we see it? Usually not directly, but we know it's there. Why? Because we do no formal advertising. That's right...NADA!! All our business is generated from word of mouth, a good part of which comes from social media. So don't let anyone tell you that it's not worth the time to join your clientele on the social networks, just do it the right way and you'll be rewarded handsomely for the effort.

When I say we do no advertising, I need to explain that we DO place some ads on Facebook and have tried placing ads on Google. By ads I mean posts that we want to hit a larger than normal market. These are not ads persay but expansions of posts for special events. To date, our experience has been somewhat mixed. Facebook ads seem to generate some additional action. However, the jury is still out on if they justify the ROI. Google ads have not proved to generate enough activity to justify their expense. In all fairness to both programs, we have used a professional social media firm who might assist in positioning the ads to maximize our exposure.

Where... What... When

As most of the Crumbzz enthusiasts who follow my posts know, I am a big believer in PR over traditional advertising (ad placement). With that in mind, I thought you would be interested in a recent PR article we posted with the media. It's an excellent study in getting the word out on your company in today's media fragmented world.

Several years ago, I had a woman come in to my bistro who asked for two cakes to be delivered one to each of her brothers. On each cake she asked that we include a gift card that would say the following:

I'm not quite sure why we have not talked in so many years. If it is my fault and I have offended you in any way, please accept my apologies. Love, Your Brother.

She explained to me that her two brothers had been feuding and not talked for over 30 years. Now that they were over 70 years old. She was afraid that one of her brothers would die before they made up and then the surviving brother would regret that decision forever. She was hopeful that by sending cakes to both brothers and making it look like they each sent the cake to each other, it might get them to talk.

I waited three months until I finally saw her again and she stated that, once they've received their cakes one of the brothers called the other. Within a few minutes of the call, they realized that neither one had sent the cakes and quickly figured out that it was their sister who had made the effort. After a laugh on both sides, the ice was broken. Although they weren't yet the best of friends, they were now talking to one another on a regular basis.

I loved this idea. It was such a "feel good" thing to do. I sat down with my team and discussed how we could offer this. We soon realized that, although we could easily do exactly what my client had done, since we don't advertise, per se, I did not have a vehicle to let people know about the program. It took me several sleepless nights to figure out a way around that challenge. For whatever reason, I have been known to wake up in the middle of the night (always around 3 am) with some of my best ideas. Because of this, I have always kept a pad and paper (now my iPad) on my night table. And, that is exactly what happened. It was at 3 am one morning that I realized that the answer to my challenge was "Diplomacy Cakes!"

We would begin sending out cakes to world known figures who are in the middle of a dispute. With each cake we would include a gift card made to look like it came from the other aggrieved party, suggesting that they get together to discuss their differences. We would not restrict our gifting to political parties but would send them to anyone who made the news. In corporate America we sent cakes to Apple's Steve Jobs and Microsoft's Steve Ballmer; GE's Jack Welch and media's Phil Griffin, president of MSNBC; Roger Ailes and

Gretchen Carlson of Fox News; In Hollywood we sent cakes to Charlie Sheen and Chuck Lorre; in the sports world, Shaquille O'Neal and Kobe Bryant received our cakes; In the music business we sent cakes to Taylor Swift and Kanye West; politicians included President Barak Obama and Speaker of the House John Boehner, House Speaker Nancy Pelosi and POTUS Donald Trump, and of course then candidates Trump and Clinton and the now President Trump and his multiple feuds (A common joke among my staff is that we need to stop sending cakes to President Trump every time he has a feud because we now believe he feuds just so he can get a free cake!).

The cost for this program is our cakes, packaging and shipping. We get no monetary benefit in return. On the surface, this might seem like a financially foolish move. But, there is always ways to find value, EVEN if it's not immediate and/or financial. Sometimes that value can be much greater than the money we would receive from a two cake sale. You see when we send out those cakes, we also send out a PR piece to the media. On occasion, we may get some local media coverage but usually, they're not picked up by the national media. But every once in a while you strike gold!

A case in point is our Diplomacy Cake mailing to two major political rivals that were continually in the news.

When we sent these cakes, as always, we posted the following news release:

Is there a simple way to get Putin and Ukraine's President, Petro Poroshenko to agree on something? Chef J Stephen Sadler of Crumbzz thinks so.

With the recent events in Ukraine further highlighting the increasingly frosty relationship between

Russia and the U.S., diplomats from both countries are looking for any areas of mutual agreement. Chef J Stephen Sadler, the Executive Chef and owner of Crumbzz, an artisan crumb cake provider from Dallas, Texas, thinks he has the answer. "Instead of breaking bread together, I say, let them eat cake". And Chef J Stephen puts his money, or in this case his cakes, where his mouth is.

For the past several years Chef J Stephen's company, Crumbzz, has been shipping his artisan created old world cinnamon streusel Crumbzz artisan crumb cakes to warring factions around the world. "There may be disagreements that can't be bridged, but everyone loves homemade Crumbzz artisan crumb cake and if you can get warring parties sharing in even one thing, that's a start", says Chef J Stephen.

This isn't the first time Crumbzz has shipped their diplomacy Crumbzz artisan crumb cakes to disagreeing parties. Obama has been the lucky recipient three times, House Speaker John Boehner and Senate Majority Leader Harry Reid have each received two Crumbzz cakes as well as Senate Minority Leader Mitch McConnell and House Minority Leader Nancy Pelosi, who have each received one.

Crumbzz does not restrict the gifting of its diplomacy Crumbzz artisan crumb cakes to political parties. Corporate America is well represented by Apple's Steve Jobs, Microsoft's Steve Ballmer and GE's Jack Welch, media's Phil Griffin, president of MSNBC and Roger Ailes Fox News Channel CEO have also received cakes. Even Hollywood and the sports world have received their share including; Kobe Bryant, Charlie Sheen and Robert Downey Jr., to name just a few.

In an interesting twist, Crumbzz attaches a gold leafed gift card with each diplomacy Crumbzz artisan crumb cake stating that the cake came from the warring party and suggesting that they get together to discuss their differences. Lately, Chef J Stephen has been rethinking his policy of sending his cakes to warring factions. With just a hint of sarcasm, Chef J Stephen states that "We may be fomenting world turmoil by encouraging world leaders to create an issue just to get another free Crumbzz Cake. Maybe in the future, we'll send them a note stating that they'll get their cakes once they settle their issues."

Nonetheless, Crumbzz will be at it again, with its recent gifting to Russian President Vladimir Putin (his second cake) and Ukraine's President, Petro Poroshenko (his first). Add's Chef J Stephen, "Hopefully they will read their cards and, call each other and start their conversation at least about how much they enjoyed their cakes".

A funny thing happened with this release. The headline "Crumbzz Artisan Crumb Cakes Sends Diplomacy Cakes to Vladimir Putin and Petro Poroshenko" along with a picture of our gift cakes, hit the Thomson Reuters big screen in Times Square!

What happened from there is true grass roots marketing at its best. With little or no marketing budget, one press release caused our phone to ring off the hook. People from across the country wanted to know how they too could send a pair of Diplomacy cakes to friends and family members who were in dispute.

Don't get me wrong, not all calls are for orders. We get plenty of emails and letters from people who think its a great idea and just as many who think we're crazy. We've also gotten some wonderful letters from folks, thanking us for providing a tool to help them break the ice. But, the bottom line is, we're getting plenty of attention from many folks who had never heard of Crumbzz before our release. To assure we maximize our coverage of this event, we even sent a follow up press release letting the local media know about our fortunate placement in the heart of New York City.

What made this release so newsworthy? Key words is the simple answer. No one cares about a crumb cake like we do. And believe me, although your product may be the highlight of your life, unless it's another smartphone, no one will care about your product either. But key words on trending issues make news. And we used plenty. Vladimir Putin and President Obama, House Speaker John Boehner and Senate Majority Leader Harry Reid, Senate Minority Leader Mitch McConnell and House Minority Leader Nancy Pelosi, Steve Jobs, Microsoft's Steve Ballmer and GE's Jack Welch, Phil Griffin, president of MSNBC and Roger Ailes Fox News Channel CEO, Kobe Bryant, Charlie Sheen and Robert Downey Jr. and of course Petro Poroshenko the President of Ukraine, were all mentioned. Each one of those names is trending and is picked up by thousands of media sources. You must stand out from the pack to get attention. In our case, sending Diplomacy Cakes fits our brand, is produced at minimal cost for potential maximum return and is, to be quite honest, fun to do.

Luck... I Don't Think So!!

In the previous chapter on our Diplomacy Cakes, I spoke about how we made something pretty special out of a chance happening. Many would call this LUCK...I DON'T THINK SO!!

I believe the word "luck" is used by those who never take a chance, never look for opportunities, in many cases and for a multitude of reasons, are afraid to stick their neck out.

I believe people who explain away other peoples success with the words "they were lucky" use that word as a shield to defray their own shortcomings. What they are really saying to others AND themselves is "if I was that lucky, I too would have done what they did, but because I'm not "lucky, I never had the chance."

I regularly provide personality profile seminars to companies, schools, organizations and consumer groups on personality types. These seminars are designed to show people how to avoid personal conflicts with others. I do this by exposing the four personality types of all people and showing them not only how to identify each persons personality but, MORE IMPORTANTLY, who THEY are. Accordingly, I understand that certain personality types are born risk-takers and other types are much more conservative. I understand that it will ALWAYS be harder for the conservative personalities to take a chance BUT, they will ALWAYS get just as many opportunities as the risk-takers and can always choose to venture out from their comfort zone if they decide to do so.

My father had a picture on the wall behind his desk of a turtle stretching its neck way out. As a child, I always liked the picture because it was a turtle. As I grew older, I appreciated that picture so much more because of the saying beneath the turtle which said:

"BEHOLD THE TURTLE...IN ORDER TO MOVE FORWARD, IT MUST FIRST STICK ITS NECK OUT."

You can call it luck, chance, Karma, whatever you want but, although they may diffe, I believe that we all get the same amount of opportunities in life. The difference between successful people and those afraid to take a chance, is that successful people understand that the opportunity in front of them may never come again and IF they are willing, they can turn that opportunity into gold! When I say gold, that does not always mean financial. Opportunities come in many forms. Not all will make you a financial success. Many will make you a personal success. By personal success, I mean a happier, more fulfilled person.

In my world travels to South America, I learned of an interesting misconception that people from the USA have of themselves. I was often politely corrected when I said "I'm an American" or "I'm from America". Whenever I said this, they responded with "so are we". I quickly learned that we are all from the Americas! I now conciously use "the States" or "the USA" when I tell new friends from other countries where I am from. Like I began to say, success in the States, is measured by the car you drive, the house you own, the position you hold and the money you have. In the rest of the world, at least in those parts of the world that I have visited, success is measured by the amount of friends you have.

Unlike in the USA, where many people identify themselves by their career, to the rest of the world, a job is simply a way to make enough money to spend time comfortably with friends and family. Unlike in the USA, where we blow in and out of our lunches because we need to get back to work. Because we are so focused on our job being who we are, we're afraid to take vacations because the person below us just might do a better job than us while we're gone and we might lose our position. People in other countries take 2-3 hour lunches with friends and family. Many take month long "holiday's" because they value family and friends more than careers and money.

The long winded point I am making is that "success" doesn't have to be monetary. It can be personal satisfaction. It can be the stockbroker who chucks it all because she loves to paint; the middle manager stuck in a job they hate, who decides to start their own little company.

My dad used to say *"Seventy percent of our lives are spent on the job. Don't be lying on your death bed and realize that you hated seventy percent of your life because you chased the dollar."*

Do what you love, love what you do, and when those "opportunities" come up, be a turtle!

Considering a Culinary Arts School... Maybe Not!

As a restauranteur, I have hired many newly "minted" chefs directly from culinary schools usually through an internship program. In every case, culinary students find their biggest challenge to be timing and pressure. They have the knowledge to create dishes from scratch (a valuable tool for an Executive Chef) but can only understand the pressures a commercial chef faces by working in an actual commercial kitchen environment. Don't get me wrong, I continue to view the hiring of culinary students through intern programs a valuable tool and continue to find qualified students who continue to advance in their career at our bistros and bakery. However, my first hand experience is that, despite all those newly learned skills and knowledge, only one out of three will make it in the industry.

If you are considering becoming a "commercial" chef, before you spend all the money, you need to ask yourself three key questions that will tell you if you are right for the chef position.

Question One – Do you thrive under "blow and go" pressure and love having new challenges thrown at you from left to right? A yes answer allows you to move on to Question Two.

Question Two – Can you maintain a clear mind and balanced personality with the ability to inspire people to push themselves to the limit day in and day out? If you answered yes, fantastic! Move on to Question Three.

Question Three – Can you consistently produce quality dishes that not only taste great but also look fantastic time after time?

If you have answered yes to these three questions, you may just be chef material.

Now you can move on to becoming a chef.

Culinary school is a valuable (but not necessary) tool if you plan to move into the industry. It provides you with valuable knowledge on the "how to" of creating and in some cases, serving dishes. It will also give you a pretty good idea if you want to be a savory chef (cook) or pastry chef (baker) two very different professions.

Working in a commercial kitchen is a "required" tool to get in and move up in the industry. And we're not talking in a chain, which will only teach you how to heat up and serve food (Can you say "Head Heater Upper.")

If you plan on making this your career, it's better to start out in prep for free (if necessary) in a fine dining restaurant than to join a chain restaurant, as a "head chef".

If you have answered yes to my three questions, get into a fine dining restaurant doing anything you can. Watch, listen and learn. Move up through the ranks. Experience is a more valuable asset than culinary school at this stage. Don't get me wrong, culinary school is a valuable arrow to have in your quiver, but experience is the bow. It will tell you if you're cut out for the business, what area you excel in, all while providing you with added chits for your resume.

Think of experience as the cake, culinary school as the frosting. It should be the finishing touches to position you in a very rewarding industry that, although extremely challenging, is also extremely rewarding. Good Luck.

Hiding The Bake House

THE BAKE HOUSE

Now that I had expanded into my retail bistro location in Forney, it was time to move out of my cottage baking location into a new home where my soon to be hired team of bakers could bake cakes, undisturbed for sales made from my website, for consumers and corporate business. Just like the wizard in the Wizard of Oz, I wanted to hide the magic we crafted behind the curtain.

Why? Simple, I did not want it to be a place where we would be disturbed by retail sales. Those could be made in Forney. I was so worried about folks finding my bake house location that I built it in an unmarked, plain brick building just south of downtown Dallas only a block away from my first home at the Ambassador Hotel.

By having complete privacy, I could build a team that would work orders received from Tuesday through Friday, 5-days a week. My staff would be solely focused on orders that were received in an orderly basis. Tuesday's through Thursdays my pastry chefs would bake cakes,

Wednesdays, through Fridays, my packing/shipping team would package and ship the freshly baked shapes made by my pastry chefs across the country.

Since I was working from a blank canvas, setting up my commercial bakery was much easier than the design and setup of my bistro. Design work was completed within 30-days, build out was completed 30-days thereafter and installation of equipment was completed within the next 30-days. We were in business within 118 days from the signing of our lease. Not bad at all. Now all I needed was employees. Not a problem...NOT!!!

Staffing... The Real Challenge

WHAT I LOOK FOR IN AN EMPLOYEE

My hiring technique is based more on attitude than capability. Experience has taught me that I can always teach someone how to do the task, I can NEVER teach them attitude. You either have the right "can do" attitude or not. I believe attitude, if learned, is learned at an early age. I personally have never met someone who was able to change their attitude once they reach adulthood.

There is also one key phrase that sets me off. Everyone in my company and my family knows it well and that is the phrase "That's Good Enough." To me, that's good enough tells me it wasn't the best you could do. It say's you could have done better. I can assure you that every one of my team members knows that it's a phrase that is never uttered in my presence.

When hiring someone new, I love to follow Angela Ahrendts strategy of asking key questions that are not the normal questions an Human Resource person would ask:

ME vs. WE

I want to understand how they see themselves in the world.

- Do they have a big ego and what role does does that play in their everyday life?
- Do they put all their energy into being an individual contributor, or do they put more into connecting and enabling the group?
- Do they care more about their own success or about the success of the team?

I'll then go on to ask basic questions about their family, friends, peers, personal interests, sports, spirituality, and community to get a better understanding of their base motivation and leadership qualities.

I'll see how the potential employee responds to these two quotes:

A famous writer once said, *"When ordinary people connect, extraordinary things can happen."*

Gary Hamel, was once asked, *"How will you know if you are a great leader?"* He replied, *"Turn around and see if anyone is following you."*

IQ vs. EQ

Now that the interviewee is comfortable and their guard has been lowered, you need to understand how they naturally navigate in the world.

- Do they typically think or feel first?
- Do they instinctively use their head or their heart?

I'll then ask a few relevant business questions about how they handle challenging situations and optimize opportunities that are presented to them. And I'll ask what their team and peers would say about them. This helps me gain deeper perspective on how intellectually and emotionally balanced they are in their life.

Once I have satisfied that they know what they are doing for the field I am hiring them for, it's important that I am comfortable that they fit our corporate culture. Are they empathetic, compassionate, caring and giving of their mind and heart?

I love the quote from Maya Angelou, that Ahrendts states should go through your mind when considering a new hire. It is what I feel goes to the heart of the Crumbzz "experience" and accordingly is a great question to be thinking about when speaking to your potential employee:

"I've learned that people will forget what you said, people will forget what you did, but people will never forget how you made them feel." You want to sense if they truly care about the impact they make on people.

LEFT BRAIN vs. RIGHT BRAIN

You should then go a little deeper to discover what lens they look at the world through.

- Do they lean into analysis or their instincts? Do they get into details, or carry on a more conceptual conversation?
- Do they make linear decisions, are they a creative thinker, or do they use their whole mind?

This is particularly important in my world because pastry chefs are traditionally left brain (analytical and methodical) driven people. Conversely, savory chefs are predominantly right brain (creative or artistic) people.

Ahrendts goes on to say *"Then go back to asking more personal questions, as you'll find that you can better assess their left brain-right brain balance by understanding what they studied, what they do in their spare time.*

- *What do they read, watch, listen to?*

• *Do they light up when talking about the arts, their kids?*

A company's success is predicated on you putting the right people in the right place at the right time. You know what you need, and you need to find out who they truly are so both can thrive over the long term."

YESTERDAY, TODAY, TOMORROW
"Lastly, learn what guides them in the world, or frames their reference points."
• How much do they look to the past to see what worked, and do they understand the forces impacting our business today?
• Do they have an opinion on the future of our field and how do they plan to evolve to keep pace? Are they averse to change or do they thrive on change?

Ahrendts finally closes with *"before they leave, it is important to let them know how you feel. If you loved them, tell them so and say you look forward to continuing the conversation. If they are not right for the position, it is best to be honest while you are together so they don't get their hopes up. Always treat them as you want to be treated, and make sure they leave feeling positive even though they are not right for the current position. It is important we all sleep at night and that they leave with respect for themselves and the company. Good luck.*

Ahrendts last quote *"Building a brilliant team is your job. Nothing you do is more important or adds more value"* is key in my mind because, without a team, all focused on the same goal, moving forward at break speed becomes a slog in the mud.

WHO AM I... WHO ARE YOU... WHERE DO I FIT?

If the potential team member gets past all the above, I then ask them to complete a Personality Profile. This is a profile test that I have taught, through my seminars across the country for small firms, family groups, organizations, schools and Fortune 500 companies. It is based on the DISC Personality program which states that every person fits into one of four different personality types. Each personality type has different values and challenges that they bring into a group. The value of knowing the personality type of each person who is a part of my team is not only for me and my fellow team members but, more importantly for the individual taking the test. I can't count the times I have heard the statement, "now I know why I do that" or "now I understand why I don't get along with _____."

Now that I know where our new hire fits in, the next step is teaching our new team member our values and primary driving goals. In teaching, I look for someone who ask's questions, repeatedly if necessary, to assure they've got it right. I refuse to work with someone who says they've got it when they don't! That person I can never trust to perform the task right because, they are usually unwilling to learn, or worse, too proud to say they don't know. I am a true believer in the fact that "first impressions are everything in teaching." If you teach your new team member the right way the first time, it will stick with them throughout their career. If you let them slide and or do a "good enough" job, that too will be their guiding force.

BUILDING MY STAFF

In New York, I had no problem finding an ample supply of kitchen and serving staff. How hard could it be in Dallas! Well, as it turned out, THAT would be a lot harder than I had planned and to this day staffing still poses the biggest challenge I have in fulfilling my corporate goals.

Staffing in my New York bakery, deli/cafe misled me into thinking staffing in Texas would be a breeze. Staffing in New York was actually pretty easy. With all the trades throughout the city, bakers were every where. Because of the large influx of immigrants, kitchen support staff was also easy to find. With New York filled with "potential" struggling broadway actors, servers were even easy to procure. In fact, I would encourage my servers to break out into the latest broadway songs and or current play skits while they were serving. These impromptu "breakouts" were not only popular with my employee's but also proved to be a big draw for my guests. The Texas market would prove to be much different!

Since I started baking my cakes in Dallas in the Ambassador Hotel first, and then eventually in my commercial bakery one block away, staffing was the first area that I concentrated on. Staffing in any company is a delicate balance of not enough and too many. When I first started out in Dallas, it was just me once I moved into the commercial kitchen of the Ambassador House I now had the capacity to grow and that's exactly what I did. As I grew I continued to add additional staff. Unfortunately, the cake gifting business (which at that time is what I primarily focused on) is very seasonal. You get giant waves of orders during the holidays and few in between. And so, my first challenge was to find temporary staff to cover during peak periods.

Most people want full-time employment and locating staff to work only for for 6-7 different holidays was no easy task. I knew that I wanted to build a "stable" team and that meant, in most cases, full time employees. My first hire was one of those fortunate events that always seem to happen when you need them most.

This is one of those "Wasn't he lucky" times that I talked about in my chapter on luck. I have been told many times in my life, how lucky I am to have had this or that happen. BUT, I am not a believer in luck! So many times I hear *"he's so lucky, if that hadn't happened, he would have never experienced that success!"* I believe that luck can be defined as seeing an opportunity, jumping on that opportunity and making it a success. So many people see the opportunities but fail to make a move. To me, *"LUCK is making the move."*

While training at a party that was featuring my cakes, I met a young aspiring pastry chef in training. We discussed the history of my family cakes, where I planned to grow and my focus on providing an "experience" versus a "product" for each of my clients. She fell in love with the product and wanted to be a part of our story going forward, and I agreed on the spot, to bring her in as my first employee. I was fortunate that since she was still attending culinary school she was only able to work part-time.

Bringing on your first employees is always a terrifying experience for a new small business owner. You are now responsible for the livelihoods of not only your employees but also their families. They are committing to provide you with their talents and hard work and you are committing to secure their livelihood and family stability. What if business slows down? Are you ready to lay someone off who committed to you? Can you trim their hours if they really need full-time work? Are you ready and or financially capable to carry them until (IF) business picks up? All of these questions run through your head as you make that hiring decision.

I never had a problem letting someone go if they were not doing the job, had a poor attitude or were not committed to making the best of the best. I ALWAYS had a problem letting a "good" employee go because business was not good.

My first employee also brought something else to the mix that was extremely important to the growth of my business. She brought contacts! Her school attendance meant that I would have a steady stream of up and coming pastry chefs to fill in whenever needed. From that initial contact, I was able to fill my erratic needs and eventually staff my entire operation.

Today I have six pastry chefs who work Tuesdays - Thursdays making cakes in my Dallas Bake House. Of those six pastry chefs, four are from those original school contacts.

Staffing for my shipping and packaging team was also fairly easy AND helped fulfill one of my passions. As I have mentioned many times, it is great to be a success and make a lot of money BUT, being a success is REALLY what you do with that money once you've made it. You may recall a quote by Thornton Wilder that I have used previously in this book. It is one of my favorites and it was highly relevant at this time. *"Money is like manure; it's not worth a thing unless it's spread around encouraging young things to grow."* I was able to help young things grow through my partnership with The Bridge.

The bridge was a Dallas homeless shelter that was located just one block from my bake house kitchen. I knew instantly that this was where I would find my shipping and packing team members.

Many homeless people actually want to work but because they have no transportation, are unable to get to a job with any frequency. With my location being one block away, that would not be a problem. And so, I worked a deal with The Bridge to hire homeless people who wanted to better their lives through a career.

As long as they held the same ideals as I did, as long as they were focused on making that "experience" for everyone of "our" clients, they would be a part of my team. Although I went through a few misfires, who really only wanted drinking money, I eventually settled on two employees who are still with me today. During that time, they have had stable employment that has enabled them to put a roof over their heads and food on the table, AND they are two of my most caring, stable employees.

THE FORNEY INTERNATIONAL BISTRO

Most people don't realize that staffing is the hardest thing there is in the restaurant business. The ebb and flow of entering and exiting employees is a constant in the business and my little bistro would prove to be one of the hardest to build a cohesive team.

Forney is a small town, located twenty three miles east of Dallas, Texas. When I opened my bistro there, Forney had around 13,000 people. It was a mix of young professionals who worked in downtown Dallas and the old guard who had lived in what just a few years prior was a sleepy farm town.

It's downtown was typical of many small towns in Texas that had been decimated by the rush to the new highways that sped people outside the downtown area to the shopping malls in the city. Although its downtown was a picturesque historic downtown, it was inhabited by only services industries: a lawyer, accountant, insurance, a few beauty shops, and a pizza joint.

Our mission was to be the first "destination" business that would begin to once again draw people from Forney and beyond back to the downtown area. This was extremely appealing to me. I would be able to bring life back to an old building and along with that, bring a special dining experience to small town Texas that was unlike anything a small town have a chance to enjoy. I can't tell you how many times people wouldn't come into my bistro and say "don't get us wrong, we love that you're here, but why are you here?" Small towns typically attract diners or coffee shops. A place where friends can meet and grab a quick bite to eat. They are not usually places where you will expect to find a fine dining establishment. This was a double edge sword for us. Half the town loved that we were there. The other half would not be caught dead in our "foo foo" establishment.

That was okay with me, I knew what my brand was and I knew who it was that I served. But, the very uniqueness of having a fine-dining bistro in small-town Texas would be the cause of my greatest employment challenges.

Interestingly, I had no problems finding well-qualified savory and pastry chefs. Remember my first hire in my Dallas bakehouse? The culinary school she went to was called Le Cordon Bleu. At the time, it was one of the biggest culinary schools in the Dallas area. When I hired several pastry chefs for my Dallas Bake House from that school, I made invaluable contacts at the school. Working with my culinary school contacts, my Forney bistro became the eastern Dallas area externship restaurant for the school.

Every culinary school requires that their students work a minimum of 90-days in a fine dining restaurant prior to graduation. During that time, the training restaurant is to send back reports on a multitude of statistics regarding the progress of their student. This externship proved to be a valuable tool that enabled me to separate the also-rans from the star players. Often times, we would wish the also-rans the best of luck and send them on their way and offer a position at the bistro to the star players. I was now well on my way to staffing my bistro. Unfortunately, finding the rest of my staff, would be the most challenging of my career. Placing a fine dining restaurant in small-town Texas is unique. In New York, when I ran an ad for qualifying servers and kitchen personnel I would receive hundreds of applications. That's not the case in small-town America.

The first challenge to being in a small town market is that there is no vehicle to locate local help. Few people read the local newspapers anymore, especially not the typical young people that a restaurant hires. Advertising on online job placement services like Monster only resulted in additional frustration. We would receive hundreds of applications only to be told, when they heard the location was outside of the Dallas immediate commuting area, that they did not care to drive the 23 miles to work everyday. Someone making a chef's wage is willing to make that trip. A person making a dishwashers wage, can ill afford to travel 46 miles round-trip every day.

An additional problem representative of small-town America is that any of the local townspeople that came in for a job, had no idea what fine dining is all about. I would receive statements like *"yes I've done fine dining before, I've worked in Applebee's®!"*

The final challenge was one of stability. In Dallas and especially New York, serving is viewed as a career. In small-town America, serving is viewed as an "until" job. That being, I'm doing this "until " I get a real job. We would spend vast amounts of time and effort training new servers, always to lose them to college and or big-city jobs.

I'm pretty proud of what my team and I have accomplished over the years. However, being able to locate and retain quality personnel, in small-town America has alluded every strategy I have employed. It is the one thing that I feel is still unfinished business.

Branding - Deciding Who We Are

Very few small business owners understand the importance of branding. My dad used to say "When you try to be everything to everyone, you end up being nothing to no one". Branding is not advertising per se, or marketing but, it should be included in both.

Businessdictionary.com defines branding as; *"The process involved in creating a unique name and image for a product in the consumers' mind, mainly through advertising campaigns with a consistent theme. Branding aims to establish a significant and differentiated presence in the market that attracts and retains loyal customers."*

When you start a new business, you have to know who you are, who you serve and how you position yourself to serve that market. You need to make sure your brand is distinct and stands out from the competition. Your strategy on how to accomplish that and how successful you are in utilizing that strategy will have a direct effect of how successful you become.

I had a clear picture of who we were. There is a high, middle and low end of every market. I believe, to be successful, you must position yourself in either the high-end or the low-end of the market. History shows us that's the middle on the market is a tough row to hoe.

If you decide to focus on the low end of the market like Walmart®, you must produce a product that is cheaper than the competition. Walmart has been extremely successful because, they beat out all the other low-end market positioned companies by producing more products, at lower prices than the competition, thereby moving the competition up to the middle of the market. If you go into Walmart® to buy a shirt you will never haggle over quality, after all, it's Walmart®. However, you will complain if the price is too high.

If you decide to focus your business on the high end of the market, like Saks Fifth Avenue® or Neiman Marcus®, you must produce a product that is superior in quality to all others. If you purchase a shirt at either Saks Fifth Avenue® or Neiman Marcus® you will expect the finest quality shirt and will never haggle about the price because, after all, it is Saks Fifth Avenue® or Neiman Marcus®!

Why not be positioned in the middle of the market? All one has to do to see the challenges of companies positioned in the middle of the market is to look at Sears® or JC Penny's®. Both companies are struggling to survive. Why? If you purchase that same shirt in the Sears® or JCPenney's® customers will haggle over not only the price but, also the quality. Companies in the middle of the market get hit on both ends! And so, I decided that we would position ourselves in the high end of the market.

Most companies price their product to a specific price point. That means, that they make sure their costs are in line so that they can make a fair profit based on what they believe they can get for the product. The cost of production, must be low enough, so that they can hit that price point. I took a completely different approach in pricing my cakes and bistro offerings.

I've chose the finest ingredients I could find. I decided that I would only use classically trained pastry and savory chef's to craft every one of my cakes and bistro offerings. I would then review the cost, add in a fair profit and price my offerings accordingly. If the price of my cakes and offerings we're more than some clients were willing to pay for that type of quality, I was willing to lose that client to the local diner or mass-produced cake producer.

At my bistro, I decided that we would cook everything from scratch, every dish, every time. There would never be the drive-in window at my bistro. I knew I would lose the guest who preferred a quick get em' in get em' out meal. and that was ok. That was the brand that I chose and it is the brand that I have successfully stuck with, all these years.

A great example of how you must keep true to your brand is something that happen to me early on. When I first started making my cakes in Dallas, I was asked by a company to private label 300 of my cakes. Even though, at the time, 300 cakes was a giant order, I told my potential client that one would not put a Tiffany® ring in a Joes Plumbing box. As with Tiffany®, I would not private label my cakes. My potential client was flabbergasted stating "you understand I said 300 cakes, right?" I required affirmatively. I lost that sale and it hurt BUT, I was true to my brand and it has served me well from that time on.

I have often been asked to discount my cakes. Something that I refuse to do because, once you offer a discount, from that point on, THAT becomes the "real" price of your product. Would you ever pay sticker price for a car? Never, Why? Because of all the sales and discounts that are offered, the SALE price becomes the real price and the sticker price is of little price setting value.

How I handled requests for a discount on my cakes is an excellent example of how to get around discounting. My 10" round cakes were retailing for around $42 at the time. In order to satisfy this segment of the market without lowering the "perceived value" of my cake instead of discounting my product and thereby reducing it's "actual" value, I created a different segment (kind of like offering a Kia® instead of a Mercedes®). I created my Minizz Snack cakes, these cakes would retail for approximately $19. If a client could not afford my $42 cake, I now had a snack cake that retailed for a more affordable $19. By doing this, I never had to discount my $42 cake. This is a strategy I have always used and it has afforded me a great amount of success.

Being Good Citizens Of Our Pale Blue Dot

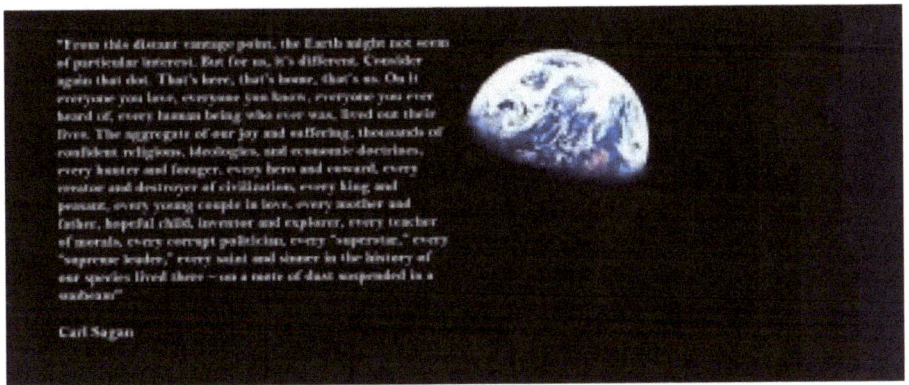

I am a big fan of everything Carl Sagan stood for. To me, it is more important than anything else we do. If you're not familiar with Carl's thoughts, visit You Tube at (https://www.youtube.com/watch?v=wupToqz1e2g) and watch his discussion on our Pale Blue Dot. I was a believer of leaving as small a footprint as possible long before the rest of the world caught on to climate change.

Back in 2000, in my first deli-cafe, I refused to use milk that had Bovine growth hormone. At the time, my supplier thought I was some kind of nut. I have always felt that the less chemicals we inject, spray or ingest the better off we all are. Yes I run all my dishes by a nutritionist to assure they are as healthy as possible. I keep all chemicals out of every dish I produce.

Although that is important to me, I also extrapolate that into being a caretaker for not only our guests and clients but also our planet.

At my bistro in Forney, I use rain barrels to water all my plants on our garden patio. I also provide 3% of my bistro profits to organizations that support sustainable farming, fair trade and environmentally sound practices. In 2018, I introduced Impossible Burgers, a burger that is made from plants. In 2019, we introduced Beyond Beef sausages, another meat made from plants and in 2020, we plan to introduce a chicken food type from Memphis Meats that is made entirely by harvesting cells instead of animals. These three dishes alone are better for our guests but even better for our planet. All of these things added up to me being able to sleep at night, knowing we are doing everything we can to be a guardian of our Pale Blue Dot. A few of the things I thought you would find of interest regarding good citizenship of our home follow. I hope they'll help enlighten you.

One Drop of Water

Did you know that one drop of water holds all the freshwater in the world? As Florencia Ramirez's book Eat Less Water states, *"If we poured all the water on our planet, both salt and fresh water, into a gallon bucket, the proportion of water available to shower, water lawns, drink and grow food, is one single drop. We live on a water planet. The earth is two thirds water, 97.5 percent of that is saltwater. Only 2.5 percent fresh*

water, 69.5 percent of that is frozen. Another 30.1 percent hides in deep aquifers. The remaining 0.4 percent – a drop in a bucket – sustains all life on this planet."

So what can we do to save water? Sure, we can drink less water. But that's not only impractical but also unhealthy. We can use less water by wiping the car down when it rains, instead of running to the car wash. We could install drip water systems for our landscaping, take fewer and shorter showers, which would help a bit…or….we could eat less water. Yes… I said "eat" not "drink".

The majority of water used by humans (seven out of ten gallons) is used to produce the food we eat and there are both efficient and inefficient methods to produce that food.

When humans migrated from hunting to farming, early farmers grew their crops naturally, in effect, their crops matched the local climate. Because they grew more efficiently, heavy water reliant plants naturally grew in wet climates and drought resistant plants grew in drier climates. But as the world population grew, methods were developed to enable farmers to expand their crops into areas less acclimated to one particular crop. And that's when we became inefficient users of our planets limited supplies of water. Water hungry almond groves in the deserts of southern California, herds of thirsty cattle in the midwest are all signs of the ever-expanding "growing zone".

All the ingredients we use at Crumbzz are produced organically. Most people would think that's because we know chemical free food is healthier and that's true. But, did you know that growing food organically, without chemicals, also saves more fresh water than any other water-saving strategy.

In addition, although some plants require more water to grow than others, that doesn't mean they are inefficient water abusers. It's not only about how much water is used but where it comes from. Water from rain is efficient, water from aquifers is limited and inefficient. So, watering the same head of lettuce naturally from rain is far more efficient than from the local aquifer. If you look at the amount of water used to make a chocolate bar (449 gallons) you would feel pretty guilty every time you took one bite of that sweet treat. But, if you realized that most of the water used to grow cacao comes from rain, you would feel a whole lot better. Conversely, that steak you so enjoyed at your favorite restaurant last Saturday cost you 1,851 gallons of water and most of that water came from aquifers. Ah, but it goes deeper.

We use lots of eggs for my cakes and bistro offerings. At your typical grocery store, one dozen chicken house grown eggs uses 276 gallons of water to produce. That's 25 gallons per egg! How is that possible? Believe me, it's not because chickens are thirsty critters. It comes down to all that grain they eat and the water needed to grow that grain. Now, if you buy free range eggs, produced by chickens that eat in fields grown with rain and moisture trapped in the soil, like we do, you just cut your water usage by 97%, and that's just on one food item!

So how can you become a good Shepard of your planet? Understand that organic, naturally grown foods are not only better for you but also better for your planet. But not all organic is watered efficiently. So make sure you buy your food from local growers. Confirm that your produce is rain watered or at worst, drip watered. Make sure your chickens, eggs and meat are produced free range.

Do this and you can wash that car without the guilt I just smacked down on you!

Crumbzz Chocolate Sustainable Farming Goal Hits 100%!

As you probably know by now, I am a firm believer in encouraging fair trade, sustainable farming and environmentally friendly processes. With that in mind I am proud to say that in 2017 we reached our goal of 100% sustainable farming in chocolate production.

Although I am not always successful in getting all of my suppliers to produce their product under sustainable and fair trade practices, I am continually pushing the ball forward on all fronts. That is why, whenever any of my suppliers reach that goal, I am more than happy to announce their accomplishment.

DIRECT PARTNERSHIPS

Through the Growing Great Chocolate™ program, my cocoa provider, partners up with the cocoa farmer cooperative, through my cocoa provider, enabling us to introduce good agricultural practices, improve crop quality, and of course, pay directly so that the farmers are guaranteed a fair price without having to share with middlemen and traders.

Through that partnership, each party mutually commits to work together and improve the quality of the cocoa, the farms and the living standards of farmers and their families.

TRAINING

In farmer field schools, farmers are taught about the complex cocoa processes, from soil management to bean fermentation and drying. The result is clearly visible: crop yields have been increasing year after year. Furthermore, yields of top-grade cocoa beans are rising – the grade Crumbzz requires for its Chocolat de la Terre Crumbzz cakes and Minizz snack cakes.

PLANTING NEW TREES

Understanding the importance of planting trees, my cocoa provider has established tree nurseries, where they grow cocoa trees and the taller shade trees on which cocoa trees depend to mature properly. Cocoa farmers can buy seedlings of both types at a low price and plant both for tomorrow's cocoa and ecological diversity.

What exactly do the farmers learn?
In farmer field schools, farmers in the participating cooperatives are trained on better cultivation methods

and agricultural practices. Member farmers learn integral aspects of cocoa farming such as:
- healthy soil management techniques
- switching from monoculture to mixed cultivation
- rejuvenating the plantations with new trees and grafting techniques
- minimizing chemical use
- natural pest control
- weeding and pruning
- tree rejuvenation
- crop diversity.

Sound production is the first step towards growing quality cocoa, and improving the crop quality and quantity in these countries sustains both the crops and farmers' cocoa growing.

How do we guarantee that the price we pay for the cocoa beans is fair?

The cocoa farmer cooperatives can sell their crops to the highest bidder on the market. In this way they get the best price for their cocoa beans. It also allows them to invest in equipment, logistics and other integral elements of the process.

I am proud of the accomplishment my cocoa provider has made in putting together a program that satisfies the Crumbzz fair trade and sustainable farming mission.

Saving Our Planet, One Meal At a Time

We talk a lot today about climate change and how it's affecting our climate and eventually us. Whether we are able to make it through this issue has a lot to do with the gasses we are putting into the atmosphere. What initially comes to mind is automobiles, utility plants and chemical pollutants. But, what most don't realize is that more than anything, this depends on what we eat. We have gone so far that even if we cut our consumption of everything else to almost zero we will still drive earth living systems to collapse, unless we change how we eat.

All the evidence now points in one clear direction and that is a crucial shift from an animal-to a plant-based diet. A recent report published last week in Science revealed that meat and dairy production are much more harmful to the natural world (and our climate) than growing plant protein. the report showed that animal farming takes up 83% of the world's agricultural land, but delivers only 18% of our calories. A plant-based diet cuts the use of land by 76% and halves the greenhouse gases and other pollution that are caused by food production.

The report goes on to state that the environmental impacts of converting grass into flesh, "are immense under any production method practiced today". The reason is because so much land is required to produce every grass-fed steak or chop you enjoy. Even though twice as much land is used for grazing worldwide as for crop production, it only provides 1.2% of the protein we eat.

We talk about the carbon dioxide from cars but did you know that "Methane pollution causes one quarter of the global warming that we're experiencing right now," per the Environmental Defense Fund. Carbon dioxide may be the most prevalent greenhouse gas (accounting for 81 percent of emissions), but methane is much more potent. Over a 20-year period, it traps 84 times more heat. So where does the methane in the atmosphere come from? You guessed it. According to the United Nations' Food and Agriculture Organization, "livestock — including cows, pigs, sheep and other animals — are responsible for about 14.5 percent of global greenhouse gas emissions. Cows are the primary offenders, and each animal releases 30 to 50 gallons a day on average. And with an estimated 1.3 to 1.5 billion cows on the planet, that's a whole lot of methane.

How do we end this?

In addition, instead of pasture land, eliminating beef and chops would allow us to re-wild this land which would allow these ecosystems destroyed by livestock farming to recover. Recovered ecosystems have been proven to efficiently absorb carbon dioxide from the atmosphere and protecting watersheds. The land that should be devoted to the preservation of human life and the rest of the living world is at the moment used to produce a tiny amount of meat.

Impossible Burgers, Beyond Beef Sausages, and Memphis Meats Chicken are just the beginning of a revolution that we hope will change the way we eat AND caretake our world. I can tell you we will always be at the forefront of this cause, because everything we always were and hopefully continue to be will only be on that little pale blue dot we call home.

Creating a Differentiator

Opening my first International Bistro was a major undertaking in and of itself. Deciding on and then creating offerings for my new home presented a new set of unique challenges. I never wanted to be the "best burger house'" To ease the path to success, you NEED to be different and THAT is where I realized that bringing fine dining from across the world to small town America would be unique. Would a meat and potatoes crowd accept unique dishes that were out of the norm? We'd soon find out!

The menu process began several month's prior to the actual building of our Forney, Texas location.

Originally, I had planned to offer a simple menu of my Crumbzz cakes, coffees and tea's. And based on this "simple" menu, it was going to be named a Tasting Pavilion. However, the city fathers really had their hearts set on a full blown restaurant to generate interest in their downtown re-development plans. Because of this, their Executive Director of Economic Development, Kim Buttram, asked that I expand the menu to include additional dishes.

Since the town was so helpful in assisting us in our move to Forney, I decided I owed them what they wanted. We would expand our menu "slightly" to include a "few" dishes.

Because of my travels over the years, I had gathered a decent compilation of recipe's from countries around the world. Although they were years in the making and when I gathered each, I had no idea at the time I would offer them commercially, I knew that these recipe's would be as good a place as any to start building my menu.

As with everything I do, my simple vision of a tasting pavilion quickly morphed into what we now call our international bistro. With that change, I realized we would need much more than that planned simple menu to compliment our beautiful new home.

As with my cakes, I wanted each and every offering to be special and I soon realized that creating dishes that lived up to my cakes was not going to be an easy task.

The first step in the process was deciding on what dishes out of my large group of international recipe's to offer. Early on, I decided that every dish had to compliment the brand; upscale, the finest quality, no preservatives or additives and unique. I ALSO didn't want to repeat my NYC hours of 6 am - 11pm. This schedule took up ten years of my life and although I loved what I did, I wanted assurance that I would have a life outside of my restaurant. This meant that I would be focusing primarily on breakfast, lunch and brunch offerings. I decided on a Tuesday through Sunday 8am-2pm timeframe. (Based on traffic patterns, this would later be expanded to 7-days per week M-F 7:30am - 2pm Sat. 7:30am - 3pm and Sunday 9:30am - 3pm, which is the current bistro schedule).

Initially I picked sixteen dishes, plus my cakes. As I continued to travel to the Caribbean, Canada and South

America, I eventually expanded to the current twenty nine dishes. In addition, we would offer coffee's, tea's, all natural sodas and eight different side dishes.

If you are in the Dallas area and are thinking of visiting my bistro, keep in mind that our dishes are always changing and expanding and contracting due to my annual trips to bring home new offerings. I suggest you check us out at our website and view our latest menu before you visit.

Initially, most of my offerings were from Europe (hence the initial bistro name of Crumbzz European Bistro). However, as I kept expanding my travels to include other parts of the world, it became obvious that a name change was due and in 2017, the bistro name was changed to what it currently is today, The Crumbzz International Bistro.

The balance of this chapter is broken into two sections. The first section is a brief description of where I found the dishes we offer. If you are a world traveler, you'll find this section of particular interest.

Even if you're not a traveler, this brief section gives you a good idea of just what's out there and where all these wonderful foods originate.

To me, the second section is the most fun to read because it's about some of the interesting facts about several of the dishes we offer. It also covers how my team and I went about making each one of these dishes ours.

A Sampling Of Some Common Dishes We Made Uniquely Uncommon

HOW TO CRAFT A BETTER EGG

Although I use eggs from free-roaming or when not available, cage-free chickens for our Crumbzz artisan crumb cakes, eggs are pretty much eggs and there is no way we could find to make a better egg. So we set out to craft a better egg dish.

OUR EGG OMELETS
Our first domestically focused dish was a pretty logical creation from an economic and environmental sense. The making of our Crumbzz artisan crumb cakes leaves us with an enormous amount of egg whites. Adding egg-white omelets to our regular egg omelets solved not only the economic and environmental issue but, also provided our international bistro guests with a healthy breakfast alternative.

I didn't want to make the usual omelet so we start off simple, baby spinach and imported parmigiano-reggiano and we let our guests add all the other fixings.

Although all my chefs were classically trained, clearly egg preparation was not part of their training. Everyone of my chefs were all novices when it came to cooking eggs. They might know so much more than me about savory cooking but, eggs were CLEARLY not their strong suit. Because every commercial kitchen is in a hurry to get the dish out, the usual procedure is to cook all eggs over a high flame. THAT is the exact wrong way to cook any egg because, high flames result in burned (brown on the edges) eggs. I had to continually instruct my chefs to turn down to a low to medium flame. My rule, if there is ANY brown, you overcooked the egg.

With regards to omelets, there is a secret to making omelets that most people don't know and it's called the "one minute rule." Unfortunately, because every person's understanding of just what a low flame is, is different, I can't provide you with the exact time (you'll have to figure that out for yourself) but omelets have a one minute window where they go from greasy to rubbery and you MUST take your omelet off the flame within that one minute time-frame. You'll have to play with it, but once you figure out your proper flame setting, keeping to the "one minute rule" will guarantee you the perfect omelet every time.

OUR SOUFFLÉ'S
Our next egg dish was much more of a challenge. We really wanted it to be special and special meant an egg soufflé. Egg soufflé's are notoriously finicky to make. One has to be well versed in their creation to make a great one every time.

You'll notice that very few restaurants offer egg soufflé's. There are a couple of reasons for this. In America, most restaurants don't have classically trained chef's making breakfast. They leave that duty up to line-cooks. Most line cooks have no idea how to make a soufflé. In addition, in America, most restaurants are blow-and-go operations that get em' in and get em' out as quickly as possible. Soufflé's take attention and time, something most breakfast restaurants are just not willing to do. That is not only because soufflé's are hard to make correctly but, also because they are very finicky with oven door openings and closings, small temperature changes, proper bowl setups, etc. If any of these issues affect the soufflé, it will fall or simply never rise. In addition, because soufflé's take so long to make (usually around 20 minutes), if the soufflé falls or fails to rise, no restaurant wants to go tell their guest that they will have to wait "another" twenty minutes (with the hope that the next soufflé comes out okay).

From France, I had a great gruyere egg soufflé recipe and another wonderful blue lump crab soufflé from Baltimore, Maryland, but my team still had to work month's on getting our process down to where we had confidence we could produce a great soufflé every time.

In my gruyere egg soufflé our homemade béchamel was one of the keys to our success. It is light and creamy and added a wonderful silky texture. The choice of the finest "imported" gruyère and the use of only parmigiano-reggiano cheeses was another factor. There is such a difference in flavor between the finest imported gruyère versus domestic gruyère and parmigiano-reggiano versus all other parmigiano cheeses and their counterparts that we were more than willing to pay the difference in price (which is as substantial as the taste differences.)

In crafting our crab soufflés, the key was adding the proper amount of fresh crab. Fresh crab. even when drained, has a lot of moisture and too much moisture can flatten a soufflé. It took multiple iterations before we finally found the right mix to assure the soufflé came out perfect every time. Adding locally grown, fresh shallots was the final touch in producing a soufflé that I believe is second to none.

OUR QUICHE

We make our quiche in house using the same recipe I found in France. In order to make a proper quiche, you must have a pastry chef. Because we make our own cakes, we always have a savory and pastry chef on duty.

Because most restaurants in the U.S. no longer have pastry chefs, they no longer prepare their own quiche. Most quiches are purchased pre-made, frozen from suppliers like Sysco and Ben E. Keith. I assure you that the crust is going to taste like a "frozen" quiche (think frozen pizza). In addition, the frozen U.S. version of quiche is much more dense than the French version.

My quiche is one of the most labor intensive dishes we make. Making the shell and then the filling is a multi-day task, but the difference is absolutely worth the time spent. The filling of the quiche, as is the French style, is much lighter and fluffier than its American brethren.

Why have pastry chefs vanished from American restaurants? The simple answer is money. Pastry chef's used to be an integral part of every fine dining kitchen. Along with the savory chefs, they created all the dishes that required any baking. This included desserts, quiche and appetizers. Nowadays, you'll only find pastry chefs in 4-5 star restaurants. Sadly, as with so many fields that require artisans, it is a skill that is slowly being lost to time.

OUR EGGS BENEDICT

There are many versions of Eggs Benedict available in America. Our version comes from Belize. The cafe in Belize where I found this dish does two rather unique things with their Eggs Benedict. (1) In the U.S., lemon juice is used in the hollandaise sauce. Our Belize version uses key lime juice. This brightens the flavor of the hollandaise giving it a light, fresh flavor. (2) In the U.S., although there are a multitude of variations, Eggs Benedict is usually placed over ham and toast. Our Belizean version is placed over fresh made blue lump crab cakes. As with all our dishes, we make our crab cakes from scratch. As with the quiche mentioned above, most crab cakes are purchased pre-made, frozen from suppliers like Sysco and Ben E. Keith. They are really bread cakes with a piece of crab placed on top. We make sure we infuse our blue lump crab throughout the entire cake.

OUR EGG SANDWICHES

You would think there isn't much you can say about the lowly egg sandwich but, that's not always the case. In most of the country, egg sandwiches consist of two eggs usually with bacon, (although sausage is more common in a few regions of the U.S.) on white bread.

That's not how it is in New York City and the suburbs of New Jersey. There, the sandwich consists of two eggs with Taylor Ham on a Kaiser roll. Taylor ham is kind of a cross between bacon and ham. I grew up enjoying Taylor Ham and egg sandwiches and was determined to share this great breakfast with my bistro guests. In the traditional New York style, I make the eggs over easy so that you get all that great yolk. I place the over easy eggs and Taylor ham on Ciabatta rolls (for whatever reason, Kaiser rolls were not as popular as Ciabatta rolls in Texas). As an added twist, I found a wonderful Jalapeño sausage in Belize that we make exactly as I was shown (I often add little changes to make each dish my own, but with this sausage I decided that it was perfect and anything I did would only make it worse)

SEARCHING THE WORLD FOR A BETTER WAFFLE

No one in America could tell you where Belgium is (it's a European country, nestled between France, Germany and The Netherlands). —However, everyone knows about Belgium waffles and yet, that famous breakfast that graces so many of our breakfast tables has little resemblance to the original waffle that hails from Belgium. In fact, in Belgium, "Belgian" waffles (note the difference in the correct spelling) don't even exist! There are two types of waffles sold by street vendors in Belgium, Brussels waffles and Liege waffles and neither remotely resemble the American version that pales in comparison to the waffles sold all over Belgium.

Sold as traditional street food, eaten with your hands and topped with whipped cream strawberries or bananas or occasionally Nutella, these waffles are not your typical calorie-laden, American version, served with gobs of syrup. No, these waffles are good enough to be eaten alone!

What Americans eat today are actually Brussels waffles (which uses baking powder instead of the traditional yeast). These waffles were popularized at the 1964 New York World's Fair in New York City by Maurice Vermersch of Brussels, Belgium. His waffles were largely based on a simplified recipe for the actual Brussels waffle available in Belgium. When Vermersch realized that most Americans couldn't identify Brussels as the capital of Belgium, he decided to change the name to the Bel-Gem Waffle which was later further Americanized to be called the Belgian Waffle. And THAT is how we got the name that we use today.

Most restaurants won't make "real" Belgium waffles because of the time it takes (double rise dough waffles are as time consuming and finicky to atmospheric conditions as making bread) and the requirement to use special Belgium waffle makers that cost ten times what a standard commercial waffle maker costs. It's much easier to just call a fat "American" waffle a Belgian waffle.

OUR WAFFLES

I decided to offer real "Liege" waffles just like the ones I enjoyed in Belgium. How different are these waffles from the Americanized versions?

Everyone has made waffles and most everyone has made what Americans call Belgian waffles at one time or the other. You make them with the same pancake batter you use for pancakes.

The real Belgium Liege waffle is not even a batter but a double rise dough. In addition, "real" Belgium Liege waffles are carmelized with Belgium sugar so they don't require syrup! To make our version of the Liege waffle ours, we finessed the recipe a bit and created a cinnamon streusel butter topping. We obviously did something right because, our waffles turned out to be our biggest selling sweet breakfast dish.

OUR PANCAKES

The choice of which pancake I would offer was a sentimental one and also one of the easiest choices I had to make. My mother's family came from Florence, Italy and growing up, we had always had pancakes made the traditional Italian way. These are not pancakes like the ones you find in America. To start with, you need to know that syrup is only found in Canada and America.

Everywhere else they use alternative sweetness for their sweet breakfast offerings.

The traditional Italian ricotta pancakes I had growing up, were filled with blueberries and topped with powdered sugar and lemon butter. Our Gamberaia blueberry ricotta pancakes, named after the famous Villa Gamberaia just outside of Florence, Italy are my nutritionist's favorite pancake. Because they are mostly egg whites and have fresh blueberries and lemon (in the lemon butter), which is all healthy for you AND because they don't have syrup which, is where all the sugar and calories are in regular pancakes, she tells me that they are the "healthiest pancake you will ever have".

There are two secrets I use to make my pancakes special. The first is the use of lime sparkling water in my recipe. The lime seltzer lightens the pancake and helps it rise. The second trick is to use "frozen" blueberries in the pancakes proper. I top my pancakes with fresh blueberries but ALWAYS use frozen blueberries in the pancake. By doing this, you'll add much more blueberry flavor to your pancakes. When you freeze fruit, the cells in the fruit break down and release all their flavor and juice. Although all that flavor and juice is now out of the cells, it's still retained in the skin of the blueberry. When the blueberries are heated during the cooking of the pancakes all that juice comes out and adds a burst of blueberry flavor to the pancake. A fresh blueberry doesn't taste as robust because it retains all that juice and flavor inside the skin and doesn't disperse it into the pancake when cooked.

OUR FRENCH TOAST

My French toast doesn't come from France but from Jamaica. Two keys make it different from your typical French Toast. (1) I use French Brioche bread because it's soft on the interior and crusty on the outside, (2) I bake it versus the traditional fried (a suggestion by my nutritionist) (3) I used imported spiced rum in my batter and in my syrup. Rum is a natural compliment to bananas and and we place fresh bananas on the French toast as well as our own banana butter.

MORE OLD FAVORITES AND SOMETHING NEW

OUR SOUPS

We offer two different types of soups, a tomato basil from Italy and a French onion gratinée from France. We make our soups as they are made in their respective countries. Although it cost's us quite a bit more to produce, the difference in how these soups are prepared in their native countries and in the USA is noticeable and worth the additional cost.

In the U.S. tomato basil soup is thickened with heavy cream. In Italy, they thicken their tomato basil soup with roasted Roma tomatoes. The difference is noticeable on two front's (1) The Italian version has a much more robust tomato flavor and (2) it is 1/3 less calories.

In the U.S. many restaurants make their French onion soup with no wine or simply use a cheap cooking sherry. In addition, they will use Swiss cheese or at best, domestic gruyere cheese on top. In France, they will use a good Cabernet wine and their domestic gruyere cheese as a topping. Gruyere cheese comes from Switzerland and France.

OUR GRILLED CHEESE

In the USA, grilled cheese is a kids dish. Two pieces of white bread covering a couple of pieces of cheap American cheese. In Europe, every country tries to outdo the other with their version of grilled cheese. And, accordingly, grilled cheese in Europe is actually a delicacy. My favorite version is from Germany.

In Germany, they add sumptuous amounts of imported gruyere cheese, carmelized onions, sautéed mushrooms and nestle it in seven-grain bread. This is how I make our grilled cheese in my bistro. No need to make any changes.

Why don't they do it like that in the U.S.? Time and money. The German version takes longer to prepare and is much more expensive to produce. American cheese is the cheapest cheese you can buy. Imported gruyere is about ten times more expensive. You haven't had a "real" grilled cheese until you've tried the European's take on this classic sandwich.

OUR GRITS

Although it's just a side dish, since they are by far my most popular side dish, I felt it wise to highlight this really unusual dish. I found them in Honduras where street vendors sell them wrapped in corn Tortillas. Since there are a few too many Tex-Mex restaurants in Texas for my liking, I decided to make them as a side grits type dish. Unlike my Jalapeño sausage, where I take out the seeds, I leave the seeds in on the grits. Like the frozen blueberries in my pancakes, it's actually better to use pickled Jalapeño's versus fresh because the pickled Jalapeño's add a more robust favor to the grits. In addition, I add the Jalapeño's juice to the corn grits to really kick up the flavor.

OUR ICE CREAM

As an ice cream lover to a fault, I knew it would only be a matter of time before I produced ice cream to compliment both my cakes and my waffles. In addition, many of my guests love the idea of adding a dollop of ice cream to their soda's. And so, I set about creating my very own ice cream.

Making ice cream is a fairly straight forward process that most anyone can do. Making GOOD ice cream is another story. The key to good ice cream is in the butterfat content and in the use of natural ingredients. Finding the right method to incorporate that rich butterfat into the ice cream is key and can be quite a challenge to accomplish. Most suppliers did not provide the butterfat richness I required to make a truly superior ice cream.

My team's research also confirmed that the longer it took to freeze our product the more likely it would be to form ice crystals. The more ice crystals the less creamy the ice cream.

I eventually found a supplier that would provide us with cream that had a sufficient butterfat content and my team eventually figured out how to incorporate that creamy butterfat to get us half way there to the perfect ice cream.

About the same time my team overcame the butterfat challenge, my General Manager learned of a way to make ice cream that would virtually eliminate ice crystals. That method was called Liquid Nitrogen. Using Liquid Nitrogen to fast freeze ice cream produces a wonderfully creamy finish that can't be found in store bought ice cream.

I now had the production methods down on how to make my ice cream and so we came to our last challenge...the flavor. I knew I wanted to incorporate the wonderful flavor of our cakes into our ice cream. The flavor I eventually chose was clearly the logical choice. Vanilla is an important flavor of my signature Crumbzz artisan crumb cake and the original vanilla in my family recipe was the finest from Saigon, and so vanilla bean carried on the tradition of being the base flavor of my homemade ice cream.

But I felt ice cream in and of itself, no matter how good wasn't special enough. As I mentioned, since I knew many of our guests wouldn't want to take our cake with ice cream, I wanted to more inclusively tie our cakes in with our ice cream. To do this, we decided to heat our cinnamon streusel to create a topping. The topping and ice cream are a great combination but, I felt our newly created ice cream needed something else. And that something came about by another one of those opportune Karma circumstances.

While cooking our cinnamon streusel cakes in the convection oven, some of the crumb topping from our cakes had inadvertently fallen off one of the cakes into the pan. That pan was used once again to make the next order of cakes. When my head chef noticed that we had double cooked those fallen crumbs, she decided to enjoy them as a snack. One taste and I knew we had found our final ingredient. We would break up our crumbs into little pieces and toast them to a crunchy finish.

The end result of all our efforts became our Vanilla Cinnamon Crumbler. As with so many of my dishes and decisions, karma and happenstance again played a big role.

OUR IMPOSSIBLE BURGER

Finally, I would like to tell you about a find that I feel is where healthy eating is going. The Impossible Burger is what I believe to be the start of an eating revolution that will be good for our bodies and the planet. It is unlike anything else I have encountered and it sure got my attention.

I have always been focused on three requirements for any dish to be added to my menu:

(1) Taste & Quality First - Only the finest ingredients must be used. The dish must be unique and MUST be outstanding in taste and composition.

(2) Commitment to People & Planet - The ingredients and or product must be produced using fair trade and sustainable farming.

(3) Health & Natural Only - The ingredients must be healthy, chemical free and all natural.

I was approached by the makers of the Impossible Burger in May 2017. They said they had a great veggie burger. Initially I was not interested. It's been my experience that veggie burgers do NOT taste like burgers. They may be healthy but they DEFINITELY are NOT burgers and in most cases, are dry and lack taste.

The Impossible Burger representative assured me that their burgers were made for "meat eaters"! He went on to say that "they would have the taste and mouth feel of beef and would even be cooked rare, medium rare or well done but, they were made entirely out of vegetables." A look at the ingredient list, confirmed that this was one healthy burger.

So I was now satisfied that it was healthy. But how about a commitment to people and planet?

The facts the Impossible Burger spokesman provided were astounding! "Compared to cows, the impossible burger
- Uses 95% less land
- 74% less water
- Creates 87% less greenhouse gas emissions

The Impossible Burger clearly met my healthy person and healthy planet requirements but, now came the real test. Could they REALLY taste like a burger? We were about to find out.

We ordered a sampling of the Impossible Burger meat and began offering samples as Impossible Burger sliders at our bistro in June 2017.

You need to understand that Texas is a "MEAT" state and it's not easy switching meat eaters to vegetable based anything! So I knew this would be an excellent test.

We didn't tell any of our subjects that, what they were actually eating was not meat but, vegetables. Amazingly, every one of our tasters loved them and until we told them the actual composition of what they had just eaten, all thought they had just eaten meat. All agreed that they would definitely choose these "burgers" again if we put them on our menu.

So, on July 4, 2017, we began offering Impossible Burgers on our regular menu and amazingly, by September 2017, they became the most popular lunch dish we offer.

If you'd like to see the actual recipes for all the dishes we crafted in our cafes and bistros, check out J Stephen's recipe book, **My World On A Plate,** available at www.Crumbzz.com and www.JStephensGarden.com, Amazon, Ingram and other retail outlets.

CHASING THE SUN

J Stephen enjoying Seafood Paella in Buenos Aires, Argentina

WHERE I FOUND THE DISHES WE OFFER

The selection of the offerings was a fairly easy task. Europe has some of the finest offerings in the world and Europe was where I started. Every country has it's great little bistros and cafes, each offering their own versions of all kinds of dishes. Europe is jam packed with chefs who are more than willing to share their great creations with you. Nowhere in the world will you find chefs who are more proud of their offerings.

Central America has its own take on great dining, it's just harder to find than in Europe or the America. Unlike Europe, where every country has distinctly different dishes and the USA where every region has its own specialty, the dishes in the Caribbean, although featuring different local spices and seasonings are mostly based on rice and beans. The challenge was to find something different, perhaps not indigent but, unique nonetheless.

South America is somewhat of a cross between the Caribbean and Europe. It has heavy latin flavor (rice and beans) but also, because it was initially populated by Europeans a uniquely European take on many of its dishes. As of the writing of this book, I have now visited the southern countries of South America but have yet to visit some of the countries in the north. This will be the next chapter in my travels. Accordingly, the dishes I have brought back to my bistro are limited to that region.

Asia is also still an unfinished work in progress for me. To date the only dish I have from Asia is from Japan. Touring the rest of Asia is definitely in my plans but will have to await the completion of my tour of the America's.

We are an international bistro providing uniquely qualified dishes to match anything the rest of the world has to offer from the good old USA. America has its own take on dishes it has created, as well as on dishes from the old world and south of the border. I wanted to feature what I believed to be the best the USA had to offer.

No matter where you travel, breakfast and lunch dishes are harder to find than dinner offerings but, at least in all the countries I had planned to feature, there was ample variety of interesting breakfast and lunch dishes to satisfy everyones tastes. It's part of what I believe makes Crumbzz different. You can find plenty of fine-dining "dinner" restaurants that are manned by great chefs. Culinary schools mainly teach their students how to make dinner NOT breakfast, (that's why I had to teach every one of my "classically trained chefs" how to cook an egg properly). My focus would be on being different. I would leave the crowded fine dining dinner market to the others. I would provide a unique set of offerings. I would offer the finest fine-dining breakfast and lunch dishes that could be found, from across the world.

EUROPE

BELGIUM -
Although they are available all over Belgium, I found the "Belgian" waffles we serve at a cute cafe called Desire de Lille located in Antwerp. If you're ever in Belgium, make sure you stop in and enjoy a "real" waffle." These are not your usual waffles and deserve their own story. (You can read the interesting turn of events "Belgian" waffles took to get to the U.S. in the next section of this chapter).

DENMARK -
I found our tuna fish recipe in the town of Aarhus, Denmark. Aarhus is about 187 kilometres northwest of Copenhagen. Aarhus is a pretty small city but, it has plenty of cafes and restaurants. Most American's know of Copenhagen but, have never heard of Aarhus but, its actually a pretty vibrant college town. If you ever get there, make sure you visit The Moesgaard Museum, it's one of my favorites.

FRANCE -
The French offerings that I chose from my recipe folder included: a Parisian bruléed oatmeal that I found about 560 km southeast of Paris in the town of Annecy, a gruyere egg soufflé and two different French quiches. All found in Paris proper. I also added a French onion soup gratinée found in a little cafe about 30 minutes west of Paris in the town of Saint-Germain-en-Laye and a Grande Mariner French toast found 3 km west of Saint-Germain-

en-Laye in a town called Chambourcy. If one ventures into the French countryside, one will find great little town's with excellent restaurants run by friendly locals.

GERMANY -

I don't believe our Freiburg grilled cheese is unique to the town of Freiburg but, as the name would imply, it came from a cafe in Freiburg. Located on the western edge of the Black Forest in the Upper Rhine region, Freiburg is surrounded by beautiful wine vineyards. If you're a wine lover, it's definitely THE place to visit in Germany and for those who have had the opportunity to try it at my bistro, a GREAT grilled cheese sandwich.

ITALY -

Our Italian offerings included: Gamberaia blueberry ricotta pancakes, named after the famous Villa Gamberaia just outside of Florence, Italy (you can read my family background on these pancakes in the next section of this chapter); A Caprese salad or Inslata Caprese as Italian's call it, originating from the Isle of Capri in the Campagna region of Italy; and our roasted tomato basil soup, found in a cute little cafe in the center of Rome.

Because they are so tourist focused, I don't usually like to look for dishes in the big cities. Rome is no different. Italy is one of the few places where you can simply rent a car and travel anywhere. Wherever you go, you'll find kind, welcoming people, manning great little cafe's, each with their own twist on Italian specialties. When not on "Pausa" (think Italian for siesta) – virtually all the restaurants and cafes in small towns close, so their staff can have a break. If you're thinking of making your first trip to Europe, make sure you include Italy. It is my favorite country to visit and is truly a foodies paradise.

POLAND -
I had an advantage here and didn't even have to leave my home to add this dish to my menu. My "little Grandma" was not only famous for her family crumb cake but also for her home-cooked pierogies & kielbasa. And so, this classic polish old world dish is front and center at my bistro.

NORTH AMERICA

CANADA -
My Salmon Hash & Eggs came from, of all places, a big tourist focused restaurant, up the road a piece from the USA in Vancouver, Canada. That's NOT the usual type of place I look to find great unique dishes but, it got such great reviews, that I tried it and it won me over. We also offer a brown butter candied bacon that I found in Quebec. Most people think of Canadian bacon as those dry round things often offered in the US but, this bacon is nothing like that and I often have to explain to my guests the difference.

MEXICO -
Our San Miguel Tuna Jack Nochalette's came from our friendly neighbor to the south, Mexico. Many Americans are familiar with Los Cabos or more specifically the town of Cabo San Lucas which, is a favorite vacation spot for Canadians & Americans. Our Nochalette's came, not from a cafe or restaurant but, from a little beachside stand.

USA -
San Francisco and New Orleans may offer some great dishes but, in the USA, if you don't start with New York

City you know nothing about great food and our New York City style egg sandwiches may not sound like much but they are traditional New York fare.

Our Jalapeño burger, Roast Pork Loin, Cranberries & Homemade Country Stuffing and our Jalapeño Biscuits and Gravy are all great breakfast and lunch dishes created by my own chef's in our home town of Dallas, Texas.

One of our most popular lunch dishes is our Impossible Burger which comes from Redwood City, California a town 27 miles south of San Francisco. We found our King Ranch Chicken Casserole in a Brownsville, Texas greasy spoon diner, all the way down about as far south as you can go in Texas, before hitting Mexico.

Our Chesapeake Bay Blue Lump Crab Soufflé came from a little cafe not far from Camden Yards in Baltimore, Maryland. And, finally our Alaskan Salmon Eggs Benedict which, may sound like it came from Alaska but, actually came from one of the many dock restaurants of Seattle.

SOUTH AMERICA

ARGENTINA -

My most recent travels to South America took me to Argentina where I brought back a wonderful pan seared rib eye steak sautéed Buenos Aires style. Served as juicy steak bites that are as tasty as any aged steak, they are a favorite at our bistro. In the Recoleta area we found a great squid ink pasta that marry's rich Italian sauces and a seafood flavored pasta that is unlike any found in the US.

CHILE -
On my visit to Chile, I brought back a wonderful Portobello Morceaux dish that I found at one of the vineyards north of Santiago. It features sautéed portobello mushroom bites gloriously paired with a sweet passion fruit gravy.

ASIA

JAPAN -
Tokyo Japan, the largest city in the world, is not my normal hunting ground for interesting dishes. I usually like small towns, where you find the truly indigenous dishes. But, Tokyo is where our Japanese pancakes come from and they are a citywide favorite and unlike any pancake found in the U.S.

CARRIBEAN / CENTRAL AMERICA

BAHAMA'S -
Most tourists visit Nassau and Paradise Island. Both offer great tourist attractions, shopping, gambling and dining. But, I'm never a tourist and I'm always looking for great dishes from the indigent peoples and that is where I found our South Sea's Shrimp Taco's in a beachside shack on the big Island (Andros). This little shack was on a "bight" (their term for an estuary) and it's the only thing they served (except for beverages). They may sound like a Tex-Mex dish but, they are true Bahamian.

BELIZE -
Belize is one of my favorite countries. The waters are blue, the topography ranges from palm-lined beaches to green

mountains. I found our most popular breakfast egg dish from Placencia, Belize a peninsula located in southern Belize. My Jalapeño sausage side dish comes from Cay Caulker, a beautiful little Island that looks like a tiny fishing village that time forgot, in Northern Belize.

HONDURAS -

Roatán is the home of our most popular side dish, our Jalapeño cheese corn grits. Street vendors sell them wrapped in corn tortillas topped with a sauce similar to Sriracha. To me, Honduras, especially Roatán, is one of my must visit destinations. Beautiful Caribbean blue waters, palm trees and friendly locals make it a go to place for Americans.

JAMAICA -

Interestingly, the two dishes I found in Jamaica are not what you would think of as traditionally Jamaican dishes. My Grilled Portobello Burger which, because of the Jamaican seasoning we use could be considered Jamaican was found in Kingston, the capital. Kingston is located on the southeastern tip of Jamaica and unfortunately, is now known as the "bad" side of the Island. Not a place you would want to visit. That's a shame because Kingston has some great little restaurants.

My Banana Rum French Toast (yes I said French toast) was found in Montego Bay, a tourist town located on the northwestern side of the country. This side of Jamaica is known as the "safe" side. Although I found my French toast in a little cafe where the locals frequent, unfortunately, this is also the side where all the hotels and tourists are and as such, has lost much of its uniquely Jamaican character and dishes.

CUBA -

We not only found some wonderful dishes in Cuba but also wonderful people, beautiful beaches, great restaurants and music everywhere. While visiting Cuba we also filed a pilot for a possible TV show on my travels. We were warned that filming would be highly restricted, people would be afraid to talk to us and food would be less than stellar. We found every warning to be incorrect. We had no trouble filming, we visited great little restaurants with friendly people everywhere and found a black been soup, shredded pork and fried plantain dishes that we added to our specialty menus.

THE QUEST GOES ON

Each year I pick a few countries to visit in my quest for the best dishes in the world. My travel calendar shows Panama and the northern part of South America as my next destinations. That will complete the Central and South American portion of my hunt. From there I will be the final leg to the rest of Asia, all in the quest to find, the best of the best.

WHAT MAKES THESE DISHES DIFFERENT

I now had my recipe's but, as with my cakes, I wanted to make them as authentic as I found them and decided to source as many local ingredients as possible from the towns, regions and areas they came from. That proved to be much harder that I had thought. Because their local dishes may not be known or popular in the USA, many local and/or regional ingredients are not imported to the USA. This meant I had to become an importer of many of the ingredients we use. Thank God for the internet as, without it, this would not have been possible.

Not all the dishes I found could be replicated, no matter how I tried. An great example of this limitation is dishes I found in Hawaii. Many of the great dishes from Hawaii feature Guava and Papaya. Guava and Papaya may be great in Hawaii but, there is simply no possible way to get either to Dallas without both losing the special tastes locally picked Guava and Papaya bring.
Sourcing of ingredients was not the only factor preventing me from offering dishes that I loved. Some ingredients are simply not going to be eaten by Americans, no matter how good they are. Horse meat is found all across Europe but, Americans would be aghast if I offered a horse meat steaks or burgers. Cricket flour is extremely tasty (kind of nutty) and much healthier for you than most of the flours made in the U.S. but it will never find a place in small town Texas.

But I was eventually able to source most of the ingredients I needed to craft my worldwide offering of the dishes I had picked for my bistro. Now was the time to make them mine.

Question & Answers with Chef J Stephen

As a restauranteur and food manufacturer for over twenty years, I've been asked many questions about every aspect of the food industry. In my Questions & Answers segment of this book, I've compiled the best to provide you with an interesting peek into what a restaurateur is asked.

Do any fine dining restaurants leave dish-washing for the next day?

Although it would always be a health department violation, that isn't the primary driving force to make sure every crumb is removed nightly. Commercial restaurants are not like private homes (some homes) where they let dirty dishes pile up in the sink and then wash them or leave dirty dishes in the dishwasher until it's full. Dirty dishes, pots and pans, flatware and glasses are washed continuously during the day. With the rapid turn over of guests, staff are always in need of freshly cleaned everything. For that reason most every kitchen has a full time dishwashing staff on at all times.

In addition, if you want to be put out of business immediately, just have your guests come face to face with any form of vermin. Commercial kitchens are magnets for all types of critters. The only way to keep them away is to have a spotless kitchen where not even a crumb is left behind. At my bistro, even though they are lined with plastic bags for waste, just in case a crumb got by the bag, we even wash out our garbage cans every night.

I'm not saying every commercial kitchen is THAT clean. Some are clearly cleaner than others but, I have been in the industry for over 30 years and I have never seen a commercial kitchen leave behind dirty dishes overnight.

If you visit an establishment that you have a concern about, as a precaution, you can check on their health dept ratings (most are available online). If they fail or are continually pinged because of cleanliness issues, stay away and they will soon be gone from the landscape.

As a server, how do you not let rude customers get into your head?

You have to understand a person that exhibits rude behavior is expecting a reaction to that rude behavior. The usual reaction is poor service and a bad attitude (giving them back exactly what they gave you).

Never provide them with what they are expecting. A polite, friendly, business as usual reaction is not what they would expect.

Don't take this as personal. Think of their behavior as a game, a game where they are expecting one thing and you, as the controller of your own destiny, are going to provide something entirely different. In this battle only YOU control what YOU will do.

By controlling the situation, you win on two levels:
1. You eliminate any excuse they have to stiff you on the tip.

2. You win the battle of wits by exerting YOUR control over the situation. You, in effect, made THIER game, YOUR game.

3. Have fun, enjoy your job. Make it everything YOU want it to be.

Is there a problem in the food industry that technology could solve?

There are several challenges that technology can solve:
1. labor challenges – the restaurant industry has one of the largest and most unstable labor forces of any industry. Technology that will assist and supplant labor demands is of primary interest to restaurateurs
2. Waste – food waste approaches 40%. A fact that is clearly in need of a solution.
3. Farm to market challenges – today's consumer demands fresh, locally grown food. Systems that assist in linking local food producers with restaurants and matching food production to market demands is long overdue.

What are the most common problems at restaurants?

Employee scheduling and food cost management are the biggest challenges for a restaurant.

Making sure you're fully staffed for your projected traffic each shift is always an ongoing nightmare.

Food prices vary with every delivery. Since it is unrealistic to vary your dish prices on a daily basis, assuring your food costs are in line with your targeted profit margins is always a challenge.

Let's say I gave a restaurant my card info while booking a reservation over the phone. If I were to cancel the reservation, would I be charged? Would I only be charged if I didn't show?

Unless stated at the time of your reservation, most restaurants don't charge for a cancelled reservation.

However, if you can't make it at your reserved time, you should ALWAYS cancel your reservation.

Simply not showing up not only complicates a restaurant's guest schedules and denies the restaurant an opportunity to schedule another guest, but it also results in a charge that negatively affects the restaurants bottom line.

Most diners don't realize that, because most restaurants use reservation services to handle their reservations, there is a cost associated with every reservation made and completed.

Because reservation services (e.g. Open Table, Seat Me, to name a couple) charge restaurants this fee for every reservation made and COMPLETED through their service, and those services consider a reservation completed if not cancelled, you should ALWAYS make sure you cancel your reservation through the same system you used to make your reservation.

If monopolies are price makers, why don't they charge an infinite price?

If the price (profit) of an item gets too high, a flood of (usually more innovative and fast moving) competitors will rush into the market.

The goal of a monopoly is to keep their prices just below that benchmark.

A great example of this is the current vanilla market. Controlled by a few monopolies in Madagascar, Tahiti and México, because of cyclones and terrorism in Madagascar, prices have risen from $26 per gallon in 2015 to $426 per gallon (US) in 2017.

Because of this rapid rise in price, hundreds of more innovative companies are rushing into the market to cash in on the bonanza. This will eventually flood the market with product and bring prices back to a more normal equilibrium.

In short, unless there are extensive gating factors preventing entry into the market (e.g. excessive capital requirements, extreme technical challenges, etc.) short term excessive profits always results in increased competition

What's your best advise for a first-time waiter job (I'm a little shy)?

You don't need to be funny, outgoing or especially talented to be a successful server. In reality the answer to your question is quite simple, make your guests experience special.

How you accomplish that can be achieved in many ways, but if your guests leave feeling you made their meal a memorable experience, you will do well.

Why does restaurant food taste better?

Not sure where you eat but no one was a better cook than my mom. Her pasta dishes were second to none. Yet, dining out was always special to me. Even though home cooks can often be better cooks than famous chefs, there are several reasons beyond the actual meal that may make a meal eaten out seem better.

1. Uniqueness – First of all food offered in restaurants is usually different from what you get at home. Due to the pressures of coming home and cooking after a long day on the job, home cooks often tend to cook what they know. Familiarity of the dining experience, no matter how good the dish is, breeds boredom with the offering.
2. Ambiance – Most restaurants provide an atmosphere that is conducive to your enjoyment. Focused on making your meal special, experienced restauranteurs do everything they can to make your visit special.

Presentation, music and decor, are all designed to add to your dining experience.

3. Social – whether you are an introvert or extrovert, we are social animals by nature. Joining others as you enjoy your meal, whether they be at your table or simply in the dining establishment, adds to our need to share our experiences with others.

4. Cost – Believe it or not, paying for your meal actually adds to its specialness. The old saying *"The value of nothing is nothing"* holds true to dining out. Often, the more you pay, the more special you'll feel about your dining experience.

What foods do you avoid when dining at a buffet-style restaurants?

Everything! Unfortunately, buffets are an American invention that fits the American lifestyle perfectly. In America, dining is all about:
1. Eating FAST
2. Eating BIG
3. Eating CHEAP

In the rest of the world, eating is about:
1. Dining SOCIALLY
2. Dining HEALTHY or NATURALLY
3. Maximizing VALUE

In addition, not only is the food usually inferior in quality and nutrition, because of the nature of a buffet, you have a small window with which to eat your food at the proper consistency. This is because, buffet food is often:
1. brought out undercooked (to assure maximum moisture while it awaits a browser to scoop it up)
2. dry and overdone because not enough browsers scooped it up before it dried out

Unfortunately, American's are all about size and a buffet fulfills that need perfectly! Buffett's allow grazers to maximize the amount of food they can consume at one sitting (can you say Obesity?)

When you think about buffet's and all you can eat restaurants, you must understand the one indisputable rule of economics. Restaurants must make a profit in order to stay in business. Accordingly, in EVERY case, the bigger the offering the cheaper the ingredients.

As a restaurant owner, what is the most valuable data to you?

Customer profiles that link:
   1) Time and date of visit
   2) Dish(s) consumed
   3) Number in party
   4) Payment method
   5) Time in/Time out
   6) Reviews (if any) made online

In the food service industry, what are some tips and tricks for servers to increase their tips?

I have written several pieces on tipping but an article in Restaurant Nuts posted on 05/14/18 succinctly lays out a winning strategy on how to maximize your tips:

    The federal minimum wage for servers is $2.13 per hour, and many states use that as their state minimum wage as well. This makes having a job where your tips are the primary source of your income downright brutal. Big tips are rare, no matter if you work at a Michelin rated restaurant or at a mom-and-pop shop near your house. Relying on the generous customers who hand them out is not a good strategy if you have bills to pay. Instead, you should focus on increasing the consistency of your tips. This will lead to consistent income and give you the financial flexibility to save those big tips for something other than rent or a car payment. Below are seven ways to increase the consistency of your tips.

1. Know the menu
I know this one sounds simple, but it has many long-term benefits for your income. Customers want to know that the person serving them both knows the food and can recommend new options to them if necessary. Knowing little details like what common food allergies are in each dish and being able to pick out low-calorie options

2. Don't be afraid to make friends with your customer or regulars
Some servers just want to come to work, put food on tables, and walk out with money at the end of the shift. Those servers don't make consistent tips for one single reason: they're forgettable. Even if they give great service, are always friendly and upbeat, and know the menu inside and out, some customers want more. Don't be shy. Learn the customers names and be willing to tell them yours. People are more likely to leave a larger tip for someone they consider a friend versus just another server.

3. Work the busy shifts
Understand that working Friday and Saturday nights typically means not seeing your friends or significant other until later in the evening. But, taking home $100, $200, or even $300 in tips after the shift is a pretty good trade off. Especially if it goes toward buying someone a nice gift.

4. Sell an experience
After a while of working at the same restaurant, it's easy to up-sell items on the menu. Up-selling an experience is a whole other game. Instead of asking what kind of wine your guests want with their steak, tell them this cabernet would go fantastic with your dish. Adding more items to your repertoire will go a long way in building relationships with your customers. Remember, happy customers are always consistent tippers.

5. Be a supportive team member

Yes, you are making your own tips (usually) when you serve tables. However, you are still part of a team. Any drama going on behind the scenes needs to stay out of the dining room. Customers don't care about what Becky said behind your back. Leave them out of it.

6. Give to receive

Giving your customers something like a mint or a fortune cookie at the end of a meal can go a long way to making your customers feel appreciated. One study showed that giving just one mint after dinner can increase your tips by at least 3 percent. Two was shown to increase tips up to 14 percent. If you have a couple spending $50 on a date night dinner, that could mean an extra $7 in your pocket.

7. Train, train, train!

If your manager doesn't do this already (which they should be), there are ways for you to train outside of work. Some liquor stores will do wine and spirit tastings on the weekends. Even going out to eat and watching how other servers approach the same job is a way to training. Always try to improve your skillset. Your customers will notice your effort.

What is the purpose of the bread that restaurants give you before they take your order?

Many restaurants not only offer free bread but also, in many cases, free salad to their customers. The reasons might have you feeling manipulated by the restaurant and in some ways you would be correct BUT, there's also a great reason you WANT that bread and salad (besides it being free).

    First lets cover why they do it. Have you ever noticed that you never get free bread and/or salad at a fast food restaurant? Ever wonder why you always get chips at a

Mexican restaurant? The answer comes down to two very important things:
(1) Profit
(2) Time

PROFIT: Lets discuss profit first. Although, it does cost a restaurant to provide that free bread (or chips) and salad, it actually increases their profits because, it encourages drinking (which is where restaurants earn most of their profit).

TIME: Multiple studies show that the longer you keep the guest busy (yes eating bread and salad is busy time) the shorter the perceived wait. Because their food comes out so quickly, fast food restaurants never have a time issue. In addition, most fast food restaurants don't offer alcohol so there goes their profit potential. Accordingly, that's why they NEVER offer free bread or salad.

THE BENEFIT TO YOU: Now you know why free bread and salad is so important for the restaurant but, what's the value to you. Don't think it's because it's free because, as we all know, NOTHING is really free. You can be assured that the cost of that bread and salad is built into the charge you will be paying for your meal. BUT, one of the secrets most chefs know is that you can usually tell the quality of the food you're about to eat by the quality of that "free" bread and salad.

If a restaurant is focused on your dining experience, that bread and salad will be just as good as the main course and the dessert. If they are pinching pennies and/or are less concerned with the quality of your dining experience, they will cut corners on the "free" stuff. A good rule of thumb: if the bread and salad are great, you can expect nothing less for the rest of your meal.

I am a trained, experienced cook, chef, server, and restaurant manager, and I plan to open my own restaurant in the next five years. What are some basic principles that can help me to succeed?

Running a restaurant is much more than making great dishes. In fact the owner of a restaurant will usually spend more time reading reports, perusing financials and working on marketing. In addition, the paperwork involved in maintaining, renewing and applying for licenses, permits and the like will only add to the workload. And then there's the staff. Hiring, firing and putting out staff fires can be all consuming. In short plan on becoming a manager not a worker.

Now I don't mean to paint a bleak picture, just a realistic one.

The upside...There's plenty.

On the front side, there's nothing like getting a great review on a dish you created, guests stating that this is their favorite place, regulars who keep coming back, visitors who heard about your place and just had to visit are all a part of why you own and creating a team that works seamlessly together to produce something special, every time.

On the back side, you can't beat the satisfaction of helping provide jobs for people to feed their families, mentoring newbies with their first culinary experience, re-awakening not only your staff but also your clientele about what it's like to enjoy real, healthy food that's not mass produced by some far away chain. And if your fortunate, building a legacy for your family.

Owning a restaurant is not easy but it can be very rewarding as long as you understand what your getting into and what your part in the picture will actually be.

Why do all restaurant waiters in the USA tell me their names? They will start with, "Welcome to...My name is...and

I will be your server," but you can see the lack of enthusiasm and boredom on their faces.

The answer to your question is simple...Tips. Research has clearly shown that when a server states their name they become a real person to the guest. When they kneel down, touch your shoulder, speak to your kids, they further personalize themselves to their guests, all resulting in increased tips.

You might stiff a faceless "food deliverer" but almost never a person you are acquainted with.

This may sound like a cold hearted fact but doing these things is a win/win for all parties. The server makes more money (usually) and believe me they work hard for every penny they get, the guest feels special and the proprietor has provided a service that will assure their guest will come back to that special place that treats them so well.

Where the system breaks down is when the process is institutionalized. When chain restaurants all "train" their staff to follow "standardized" welcoming rules, they become rote and lose their meaning. Servers then "follow their "training" without thinking because it's the "rule".

At our Forney, Texas International Bistro, we ask our servers to treat people like they have just come in to visit them at their home. Do those thing that will personalize you to your guests, but do them because you mean it, as if you are talking to a friend.

Not easy to do when you have a line of guests waiting to be seated, looking for refills and awaiting their dishes. But that's the art of being a professional server. Understanding who needs attention and the attention they require is an art not process. Chains who are all about systems and controls often lose site of that fact.

Do many/any nice restaurants serve meals to a table "one-at-a-time-when hot" vs. all-at-the-same-time? What is the general restaurant trend around this?

Our chef's are all classically trained from Le Cordon Bleu. Although classically trained, when they start with us (or any restaurant for that matter) the most challenging task they immediately face is the ability to create AND provide all dishes simultaneously. This is when most aspiring chef's "wash out" (decide that being a chef is not for them).

Delivering dishes on time goes beyond one dish and one ticket. It includes the monitoring of multiple tickets all with multiple dishes. Most chef's use several timers to help achieve this. Our kitchen features multiple staff members, all gliding from task to task, reacting to multiple timers, to assure that each table is served as quickly as possible in a timely manner. Granted, we make all our dishes from scratch which only add's to the complexity of the assignment and in order to cut down on the complexity and time to provide dishes, many kitchens pre-make many of their dishes. However, the basic challenge still remains.

A great example of this is the following scenario for a seemingly simple party of five breakfast at our International Bistro in Forney, Texas: Our sample order consists of five dishes: (1) waffles, (1) pancakes, (1) soufflé, (1) Eggs Benedict and (1) oatmeal. Seems simple, right? Well let me give you a little insight into just what goes into crafting those dishes.

Our chefs know that the waffles take 4 minutes, the pancakes 11 minutes, the soufflé 20 minutes, the Eggs Benedict 4 minutes to poach the eggs, 16 minutes to bake the crab cakes and the oatmeal takes 8 minutes to cook, 1 minute to slice the fruit and 3 minutes to brûlée. In addition, our chef's are usually working multiple dishes at the same time.

This simple breakfast seems quite simple to the guest but involves a great amount of training and focus on the part of the chef. Now take that same ticket and multiply it by 20 tickets all in queue at once with some parties as large as 20 people! I believe that will help you understand what it means to be a chef and just what goes into providing those SIMPLE dishes all at once to your table.

Being a chef requires two often conflicting capabilities, intense focus as well as the ability to multi-task while under great pressure.

To assure all dishes come out simultaneously all cooked to perfection is the magic that separates the chef from the cook.

Restaurant Operators: What are your go-to interview questions for 1) front of the house candidates and 2) back of the house candidates? List your top 5 that you commonly ask.

For me, the key ingredient for front or back is always attitude. A person can be taught process. They cannot be taught attitude. Whether it's cleaning floors or crafting a soufflé, I want someone that is driven to craft a masterpiece that will assuredly provide the ultimate guest experience.

With regards to capabilities, we do follow a few guidelines.

CHEFS
For chefs, I have found that offering externships for the local Le Cordon Bleu College of Culinary Arts in Dallas is the ideal way to get classically trained chefs that have not yet formed bad habits.

SERVERS
Our biggest challenge is servers. Our fine dining Forney, Texas Bistro is in a town that does not have any other fine dining establishments. Accordingly, we have a hard time finding servers that understand the difference between food delivery (which is what you get at most chains) and fine dining. In this case, I would rather train a new server from scratch. More time consuming but more rewarding to our guests in the end.

I also want someone who has compassion for others and easily assimilates with other team members. I learned many years ago, that one employee who has a bad attitude can quickly destroy a team.

Why do some delis have sneeze guards while others don't?

Some state and county health codes require sneeze guards and some do not. In addition, some restaurants choose to install them (even if not required) to assure customers of their focus on cleanliness. Unfortunately, the only way to actually confirm a restaurant places cleanliness at the top of their list is to view their kitchen. If the food is contaminated coming out of a dirty kitchen, a sneeze guard will do nothing to prevent health issues.

Why don't the majority of customers fill out comment cards at restaurants?

When I'm in negotiations, I always draw a circle and place every person who has any part in the issue around the circle. I then go around the loop and note how each person involved benefits. If I find one person who does not benefit, I restructure the offer to assure that person benefits as well. Experience has taught me that no matter what one thinks, progress always stops at the person with no benefit.

In this example, the customer receives no benefit by filling out the survey. Figure a way for the customer to benefit and your replies will increase exponentially.

What is it like to eat alone at a fancy restaurant?

I personally like to eat alone on some occasions, especially when I'm working on business issues that I need to think through. One of the things I do hate is when hosts make you feel like a loser when they ask "JUST one?" The question makes one feel as if, you really can't find even one more person to dine with?

At our International Bistro in Forney, I always have my team ask *"will anyone be joining you?"* When the guest says no, we say *"great, let me clear these settings so you have a bit more room."* I believe this simple change makes our single dining guests feel welcome and comfortable.

What does it take to successfully go from "I really enjoy cooking" to "I'm opening a restaurant"?

A key element no one else has mentioned is $$$$$. For a decent restaurant figure a minimum of $500,000+.

We're talking buildout, equipment, staffing, stocking, advertising, menu (dish) creation, taxes, fees, cash flow, (if you're a start up, everything will be C.O.D), etc. and 1-3 years of slim to no profits.

Is it profitable to install an outdoor dining area to a restaurant?

A few factors can make the difference here. (1) Weather is one. If you're in an area that has at least 4 months of "patio" weather (not too hot, not too cold) you can extend this with heaters and misting fans, (2) age of your clientele (young professionals are better than older folks and/or families), (3) extremes are the best, park like (water view, plenty of trees and grass) or busy road (for people watching) and finally plenty of PR (throw patio parties, spring is here, events, Octoberfest, etc.

I want to open a small cafe, whilst holding onto my full time job. Am I deluded in thinking that I can do it?

Deluded in that you can do it? No. Deluded that you can do it well? Yes. Your cafe will only be as good as your employees and employees almost "never" have the same passion for the business as an owner.

If you're thinking small, try profit sharing or if you can find an employee that you really find a common interest and trust level with, make that key employee a partner based on surpassing a set of clearly defined achievement levels.

If you're thinking big, think stock options.

Either way, an employee that has a vested interest is more likely to think like an owner.

How often does a restaurant owner go to another restaurant?

I visit other restaurants as often as possible. Fortunately, my schedule allows me to visit several times a week. Although many people would love to go out to dinner that many times a week, I view this as a vital business requirement.

As a chef and restauranteur it's important to stay in touch with the market. Not only in the type of dishes being offered but also new ways to present foods, serve guests, new dining experiences in ambiance, entertainment and new ways to craft existing offerings.

In a market where new and exciting is a driving force to the consumer, the chef and/or restauranteur who isn't attuned to the market and thinks they know it all, will soon be left behind.

In addition, I also like to try to figure out what ingredients they have used in a specific dish and or how they put the dish together.

On occasions where the restaurant has an open kitchen, I watch how the chefs, sous chefs and prep team efficiently (and sometimes not so efficiently) put dishes together, how long it takes from order receipt to completion, and how long the dish sits under a heat lamp (if any) before the server brings a dish to the guest.

Through the years, I have learned a multitude of things to do and not to do, from sitting on the "other side" of the table.

By the way, understanding how hard it is to maintain high standards of quality and service in an industry as transient as ours, when I enjoy my visit at a restaurant that has it all together, I ALWAYS make sure to compliment the chefs, waitstaff and owners on a job well done.

On a side note, I also make sure my tip is representative of the service provided. Most people don't realize that most servers only make $2.15 an hour! Can you live on that? I know I can't. The rest of their income comes from tips. I'm always amazed at people who leave a 10% tip or less for a great meal and great service. If the service is good (note I said service not meal, since food preparation is usually not the servers fault), whether it's breakfast, lunch or dinner, I always leave 15% of the TOTAL bill, 20% or more for excellent service. I will leave 10% or less for poor service and usually leave a note (as a learning tool) detailing the reason for my tip. If the server learns from it, fantastic! If not, they won't be long in this position.

If you could develop the perfect food, would people eventually stop eating everything else?

To most people, food is much more than than fuel for the body. Few people eat solely for one reason (e.g. health, nutrition, hunger, etc.) My mother used to say that too much of any one thing is not good for you. The perfect food might end up being good for you but would soon bore most people. Variety is the spice of life and that includes food. Enjoyment of different foods may be based on flavor (one time you might be in the mood for something sweet, another time something savory) or on mouth feel (something soft like a parfait or mousse or something firm like ribs or a burger. Unless the perfect food could morph into ALL these forms and tastes on demand, it will never fill anything but a very limited segment of ones diet.

What are some things that people just do not understand about the restaurant business?

There are several areas of the restaurant business that most customers don't understand. Each are an integral part of making their dining experience special and not all are about preparing their dish.

Because of its multiple challenges, the restaurant business is one of the most challenging businesses to manage successfully. There are daily stories of GREAT home cooks and even classically trained chefs who fail every day. In each case these wanna-be restauranteur's fail to understand that offering great food is only one part of the equation of owning a restaurant.

Not only potential restauranteurs are fooled by what looks like a simple business model, customers are too. It's simple, cook a dish, serve it, get paid and your done...NOT!!!

Most people take for granted the effort it takes to make a simple dish that comes out of the kitchen perfectly crafted, right from the oven, every day, every time.

The reason for this misconception is because most people have a picture of meal preparation that is based entirely on home based meals. Restaurant meal preparation and the service of those meals is a completely different animal.

In order to accomplish this feat, the owner must have servers that are personable, intelligent, efficient and not afraid (or capable) to run on their feet for an eight hour shift. They must do this with a smile on their face and a cheerful voice, while putting up with screaming kids, snotty teenagers, unfairly demanding mothers and sexually condescending husbands (this can be reversed to include any sex, but is most common as stated). Unfortunately, unless your restaurant is located in a major metropolitan area, many servers view server jobs as temporary. I'm doing this until...is a common refrain heard at every restaurant. Accordingly, staff turnover and training is a constant challenge.

In addition, dishwashers, busboys and greeters are also vital cogs in the wheel of any restaurant but, because of the positions pay rates and lack of potential upward career mobility, are always a challenge to find and retain.

In order to get your dish out in a timely manner, kitchen staff must be able to multi-task and work together as a seamless team at all times. This is not as easy as it sounds. At home, you purchase your groceries based on what you plan to make and for how many people will be joining you at your table. You prepare the specific meal you plan to make, based on the time you plan to serve dinner. The main dish and side dishes are prepared so that they come out at the time you wish to serve and when complete, the entire family sits down to eat. If you are having guests, although quantities may change, the process is basically the same.

At a restaurant, although you have a general idea of how many people will be your guests at a particular time, you're NEVER really sure. Accordingly, your purchase of foodstuffs is an educated guess at best. Purchase too much and the extra goes to waste and you quickly go out of business. Purchase too little and you upset your guests, lose money on the dishes you were unable to make and...you guessed it, quickly go out of business.

In addition, in a restaurant, you may have 20 tables of four people each requesting a different meal and each arriving at a different time. Unlike at home, you DON'T have the luxury of everyone sitting down at the same time and eating only when you have prepared the meal. Each one of your dishes requires a different time to cook, including the main course as well as the sides. For one single main dish, say a soufflé, this will take approximately 5 minutes to prepare and 16 minutes to bake, your side dish of broccoli may take 6 minutes to blanch, your scalloped potatoes, another 12 minutes. That's for just ONE GUEST! Of course you have 3 more guests at that table, each with their own different dishes and that's just for ONE Table! And ALL of these dishes must come out at the same time! Now, times that by 29 tables and you have an idea of what the kitchen staff faces every night!.

At my suburban Dallas bistro, we have provided a major culinary school with the externship for their chefs in training. I can't tell you after training in a "real world" commercial kitchen, how many chefs-to-be, decide that working as a chef in a commercial restaurant is not for them.

As the restaurateur, you need to know how to staff (too many people, lose money, go out of business), too few, unhappy guests, lose customers and yes...go out of business. Do you see a pattern here?

This is not to say that working in or owning a restaurant is not a wise career choice. Providing someone with an experience they will talk about for years to come, making new lifetime friends from the people who visit you on a continual basis is a wonderful experience that is truly unique to the restaurant business BUT, you must like a fast paced, always changing environment that will require that you think on your feet and multi-task throughout the day, everyday.

As a restaurant guest you now know, as Paul Harvey used to say...the rest of the story!

Have a little compassion and understand that the great meal you just enjoyed was a symphony produced by a dedicated conductor and his symphony of staff members, all working tirelessly in unison to provide you with a special memory.

What happens if you don't tip your waiter in the U.S.?

I've read several of the replies to this answer and because they are SO misinformed felt the need to reply.
FACT 1:
Servers NEED tips to survive.
Although there are some limited markets where servers make more, MOST servers across the U.S. make $2.15 per hour. Tips are where they make their living wage.
FACT 2:
Restaurants DON'T make up the difference.

If you don't tip your sever MOST restaurants DON'T make up for the difference. The restaurant server relies entirely on the service they provide and the tips they receive for that service.

FACT 3:
The restaurant isn't the beneficiary of low wages...YOU are! Restaurants work on tight margins. Many comments state that the restaurant benefits from the low wage BUT, it's actually the customer who benefits. HOW? Pretty simple economics here. If the restaurant is forced to pay a higher wage, they will simply pass that cost on to the customer through higher dish prices. Enjoy those low dish prices? Thank your server and tip them accordingly.

FACT 4:
Servers who question customers regarding their low tip are GONE! If a sever ever questioned a customer about their low tip, MOST restaurants would immediately terminate their employment. Tips are a direct response to the service provided and should reflect that in the amount of tip provided (customers should be careful to separate delays in food and/or poor quality of food due to kitchen issues versus delays due to poor service by the server).

FACT 5:
Tips are a great tool for restaurant owners. WHY? MOST restaurants track the tip percentages of their employees. Why? Tip percentages are an excellent tool that tell the restaurant owner how well each server is doing with satisfying the customer. Servers that continue to get poor tips are usually retrained or if retraining fails, terminated.

FACT 6:
Tips are an excellent way for you to ensure excellent service. Tips are the tool that clarifies who should work in the service industry. HOW? GOOD servers make GOOD tips and tend to remain in the business. BAD servers make BAD tips and eventually leave the business. NOW you know the ACTUAL facts about server tips in the restaurant industry. Tip your servers well if they do a good job. If they don't, let them know by the tip you leave. It will either be a teaching

moment or a reward for making your dining experience special.

What is your experience with the Olive Garden Pasta Pass?

It's like getting a lifetime supply of Spaghetti O's. Great, until you have to eat the stuff!

When dining in a "nicer" restaurant, is amuse bouche served to all patrons or only select ones?

Amuse Bouche (in French it means "mouth amuser") is not very common in the U.S. When it is served, although on occasion it may be served to V.I.P's only, it is usually served to all patrons. Because it is a prelude to the meal, it's is seen as a sneak peak into the chef's vision of his craft.

Besides restaurant servers, who should I always tip?

Although servers at restaurants are the first people that come to mind when you think of tipping, most of the service industry survives on tips. Unlike restaurant servers, there is no set rule on tipping amounts for these services. Tip what you think the amount of service provided is worth and how much effort the service provider put into making your experience special.

The most common service providers that receive tips include; parking attendants, bartenders, salon and spa workers and hotel bell hops.

In addition, although they don't usually provide any "real" service, except for drinks and the provision of my bill, I also tip buffet servers (usually 10%).

Did you ever go to a celebrity chef's restaurant and leave disappointed?

Yes, although I should have known better. A couple of years ago a few of our out of town guests wanted to visit Wolfgang Puck's Five Sixty fine dining restaurant atop Reunion Tower in downtown Dallas, Texas.

Reunion Tower, in and of itself is an oft-visited landmark in Dallas. This 560-foot tower has a distinctive glowing ball at its top that revolves 360 degrees to provide visitors with a panoramic view of downtown Dallas. Wolfgang Puck's Five Sixty restaurant lies within this revolving globe. And therein lies the issue.

The restaurant itself is impressive looking. Upon ascending 50 stories (elevator assisted), guests enter through the center of the restaurant. From there on, they are greeted by floor-to-ceiling windows throughout the restaurant dining area, offering guests a 360-degree view of Dallas as the entire dining room revolves.

The high price of the dishes represents not only the Wolfgang Puck name but also the uniqueness of dining in a 360-degree revolving dining room. Although the uniqueness of the dining experience was pretty cool and the service was good, the food was okay at best.

I'm pretty picky about my dining experiences. I have no problem eating at a fast food place when that is the only option BUT, if I'm dining at a fine dining restaurant, I expect them to adhere to the three cardinal rules of fine dining:

1. The ambiance must be great
2. The service must be exemplary
3. The food must be exquisite

Clearly, Wolfgang Puck's Five Sixty fell short on the last requirement. BUT, I fully expect that they'll continue to do well. But why is this so?

Missing out on one, two or even all three factors mentioned above is a common issue with special destination dining locations. But these establishments know full well that guests are willing to pay top dollar NOT because of the food, service or ambiance but, because of their unique offering.

Whether it be waterfront dining, theme restaurants such as Medieval Times, theme park dining restaurants or theatre dining establishments, what guests are really paying for is that unique experience. This is a common issue with most special destination dining locations.

In Wolfgang Puck's Five Sixty's case, it's the revolving dining area that's the draw for its guests. When a restaurant doesn't have to rely on the three cardinal rules of fine dining, they often tend to slacken on them.

Although it's a Wolfgang Puck restaurant for heavens sake, as I was ascending into that revolving ball, I should have known better that, although I would probably enjoy the experience, which I did, I shouldn't have expected it to meet what SHOULD be one of the key ingredients in fine dining.

Would a dirty restroom keep you from dining at or returning to a restaurant?

It's all according to the restaurant type and what you mean by dirty. I frequently visit an old restaurant that would be considered a Greasy spoon type establishment. The restrooms are old and decrepit (just like the restaurant) but the food is great and fresh.

On the other side of the coin, if you visit a restaurant that is fairly up to date but the restrooms are dirty, I'll ALWAYS take that as a sign the the restaurant is poorly managed and the kitchen is probably in just as bad shape as the restrooms. In that case, I'll usually skip that establishment.

What are some example of high profit food items in a restaurant menu?

In the U. S. it's always alcoholic beverages. That's the reason many restaurants steer you towards their bar when they put you on their waiting list. The restaurant can often make more on your 20 minute wait at the bar then on the meal itself.

Why should the founder also be a brand face of a company?

The use of a founder as the face of a company can be a great asset in setting the brand identity. Because consumers find it much easier to identify with a person than a company, utilizing a dynamic founder as its face provides immediate results. Enabling consumers to identify with a company is the key to positioning the company in the public's eye.

Utilizing a founder as the face of the company is a double edged sword. On one hand, the founder can be a real asset to the company if he/she is colorful (Richard Branson - Virgin), has a direct link to the creation of the product (Steve Jobs - Apple), or is aligned with the products image (Colonel Sanders - Kentucky Fried Chicken). People like to have a face associated with a company. In addition, utilizing the founder, if they match one of the three criteria above, provides the company with a lot of room to build a story around the founder that resonates with the customer.

However, linking the founder to a company can turn into a real disaster if the founder turns out to be flawed (e.g. Martha Stewart's stock manipulation and eventual imprisonment, Papa John's John Schnatter use of the "N" word at a stockholders meeting, etc.)

Would you choose a small business with rich customers or a large business with poor customers?

Both can be successful. The key is to be true to your brand. Pick the one that best fits your product AND your personal tendencies.

Be careful when deciding your position in the market, you must be consistent to your positioning because, once you decide on where to place your brand, you (almost) never can successfully waver from that position. The temptation to vary can be overwhelming for a start up. When I started my gift cake business, I positioned my company in the Neiman Marcus strata. My packaging featured wax seals, jacquard ribbons and leather finished boxes. My company name was limited to the ribbons to avoid any "crass" low level commercialism.

A great example of what happens when you lose your brand identity is what happened to the Tommy Hilfiger brand. Initially a quality product positioned at the high end of the market, Tommy Hilfiger decided to open up its product offerings downline. Within a couple of years it became the go to wear for the Rapper crowd. Oversized, Tommy Hilfiger jackets and jeans were seen on every corner and in every club. That change increased sales to THAT market but decimated the high end market. Not one of the Neiman Marcus crowd would now be caught dead in a Tommy Hilfiger piece of clothing. For years now, Tommy Hilfiger has been trying (unsuccessfully) to get back to its high-end market roots and to date has not been able to regain the cachet it once had.

Conversely, not wanting to make the same mistake Tommy Hilfiger made, to assure they didn't destroy their brand, when Ralph Lauren went downline, they created an entirely new line (Polo) for that market.

This example can also be seen in automobiles. In order to sell their cars to a high end market companies like Toyota and Nissan had to create entirely new brands (Lexis and Infinity). Although both are Toyota's and Nissan's at heart, NO high end buyer would ever consider owning a Toyota or Nissan but, have welcomed with open arms the Lexus and Infinity brands because they have been positioned properly for that market.

So, think through very carefully your brand positioning. History has shown that once you position your brand, successfully changing markets is an unlikely scenario

What was the dish that made you reverse your opinion on a food you had until then disliked?

As a child I had always hated pork chops. They were always dry and resembled shoe leather in texture. Although my mother, who was Italian, was a great cook, especially with all her Italian dishes, she believed that pork had to be cooked into oblivion in order to be safe to eat. Unfortunately, at least for me, that safety factor made them inedible. When I married my beautiful bride, one of the first dishes she made me was pork chops. At first I didn't recognize exactly what it was that I was eating. Since I had never had pork chops cooked correctly, it seemed like I had found an entirely new dish! THESE pork chops were juicy, tasty and downright delicious!

It was at that time that I realized how important proper preparation was in maximizing the potential for any one dish. As a chef, it taught me that varying my preparation can completely change the outcome of anything I prepare.

Ever since that time, pork chops have been a welcome addition to my dining vocabulary.

Some restaurants use trays to bring and remove food and other do not. Why?

Although you see trays in most chains, fine dining restaurants don't use trays as a general rule. Fine dining are all about personal service and trays are anything but personal.

Trays are also used in chains that cater to large parties which are the exception to the rule at fine dining restaurants.

In addition to fine dining restaurants, because they cater to intimate small parties, bistro's and cafe's will also almost never have trays.

Why do people ask waiters for their opinion on certain items on the menu, when it's pretty obvious that the waiter will say that everything is good?

A well trained waiter will NEVER say everything is good. Restaurant's that know what they're doing, train their waiters to highlight specific dishes. This could be limited availability specials or dishes the restaurant wants patrons to experience AND yes, even dishes that have the highest profit.

Either way, you'll only hear "everything" from an inexperienced and/or untrained waiter. Stay away from restaurants that have either. Heaven knows what you'll end up with.

You want to experience the dish the restaurant wants you to try because, it usually is the dish they do the best.

Have you been treated differently by a restaurant server whom you noticed was serving others better than you?

On occasion I have noticed certain guests being treated special by servers. However, as a restaurateur, I never take it personally. I understand that in most of these cases it's about a guest who is a regular, especially one who is a big tipper. I also understand that this has nothing to do with me and everything to do with the relationship that server has with that particular guest.

If a server favors someone because of the color of their skin, their sexual preference or their sex, that's an entirely different matter. In that case, it's a legal matter and much more than guest preference. However, ALL of these issues are representative of one clear fact. And that fact has NOTHING to do with the server. If you're looking to place blame, place it squarely on the management. ANY favoritism, for whatever reason, is the direct result of poor management. Guest/server relationships ALWAYS come from the top down. If you have a server who is prejudiced, he or she is gone. If the server is showing favoritism for any other reason you re-train. If they can't be trained, they're gone. It's that simple.

If this isn't done, its a sign of either a poorly managed restaurant or worse, management who are complicit in the servers prejudices. If that's the case, it's time to write this establishment off. It will only be a matter of time before enough people do just that and the offending restaurant and server will be gone.

A well managed restaurant will NEVER allow its servers to favor one guest over another. If ALL guests are treated special, even that "SPECIAL" guest will continue to frequent the establishment. However, in every case, if favoritism is shown to a select few, the restaurant will lose ANY guest who feels slighted. A well managed restaurant will understand this and make sure EVERYONE is on their special list.

Do some restaurants put on a front for health inspectors?

Every restaurant wants to look its best for the health inspector. However, health inspectors are no fools. They often show up on a restaurants busiest days when restaurants have little time to cover up their issues. In addition, most inspectors know all the tricks and typical corners that violators often cut.

Put on a front? Perhaps but, fool the inspector? Unlikely.

I feel like I have a very unsophisticated taste in food and dining in an expensive restaurant is a waste of money. Is this unusual?

For years my kids drank Tropicana concentrate orange juice. Sometime in their early teens, we had breakfast at a fine dining restaurant. The orange juice we were served was fresh squeezed. My kids hated the "stuff" (pulp) in their juice. It was at that time, that it became obvious to me, that they were a product of their upbringing. Is "fresh" OJ better than concentrate? Most would say yes but, it clearly wasn't to my kids!

The point, just like ones first taste of a fine wine, most will prefer a soda or fruit juice because, it's what they know, what their taste buds are used to. Like that fine wine, fine dining is often a learned experience.

This doesn't mean that you HAVE to learn to LIKE fine dining, you can continue to enjoy what you know and what you like, without any guilt. However, understand that fine dining is definitely NOT a waste of money.

Although it's a given that fine dining will provide you with exemplary food, fine dining is not limited to the food you eat. It is the service, the ambiance, the settings, the plating and so much more. In short, fine dining is the "experience".

Can you get a great steak at your corner bar or diner, maybe. But you'll never get the "experience" that fine dining provides.

And THAT is what fine dining is all about!

Is the restaurant name "eggslut" demeaning to women?

Women no....chickens yes.

As a person working in food service, how does it feel to watch people eat for much of your day?

Your looking at what you provide through the wrong lens. At least in fine dining restaurants (my bailiwick), your not providing food. What your providing is an experience. You DO enjoy watching your guests enjoy the experience you've provided. There is nothing more rewarding then making your guests evening special.

You don't watch them eat per se but, instead watch them enjoy the experience of the food, wine, ambiance and YOUR service. That's quite a different thing then what you propose with your question.

Now, many might say that my reply is not relevant in the fast food business but, I would disagree. It you focus on the guests experience, you will ALWAYS do better financially and will ALWAYS increase your level of enjoyment at your job.

As far as the food is concerned, no matter how good the food is, after a while it gets old eating the same thing all the time and you'll soon forget about the food and realize you're actually in the service business.

What are red flags that a restaurant will have bad food?

Before you eat, check out the cleanliness of the bathrooms and the restaurant in general. Check the condition of the furniture and the cleanliness of the wait staff. If the restaurant doesn't take care of those areas, they won't be taking care of your food or the cleanliness in their kitchen.

Check out the menus, are prices updated by scratch outs, a sure sign they are operating on a severely reduced budget. A severely reduced budget often means cheaper ingredients and a reluctance to throw away food that has gone bad.

If you have already ordered, check out the bread and salad. In almost every case, if the owner skimps on the bread or salad, they're skimping on the food you'll be served.

What do the lines on the side of restaurant cups mean?

Although the lines may vary by manufacturer, the lines you see on these cups are fill lines for different drinks (e.g. 8 oz, 12 oz, 16 oz.). Usually for cost purposes, many restaurants utilize one cup for all their to-go drinks.

Although utilizing one cup may keep costs down, the restaurant needs a way to assure that drink specifications are met. A typical example may be to provide 16 oz for iced tea, 12 oz for whole milk and 8 oz for orange juice. These lines help restaurant staff pour to specifications.

What is a particular dish you always order at a sit-down restaurant just because it's that good?

An excellent start to my meal would be the classic French starter, escargot. This would be my number one choice for an appetizer. Although it may sound repugnant to those who haven't experienced this delicacy, escargot usually features Helix pomatia snails, cooked in a garlic butter wine sauce, which is seasoned with thyme, parsley and oftentimes, pine nuts. Unlike my other choices, one can find properly prepared escargot in many places across the U.S.. If you are hesitant to try this delicacy, close your eyes and open your mind and charge ahead. You will be rewarded with a great start to your meal.

My entree is much harder to find prepared properly, or improperly for that matter. I am always on the hunt for a great Canard à l'Orange (also known as Duck à l'Orange in the U. S.). This classic Italian dish, yes, I said Italian (most people think it originated in France but it actually originated in Naples), features duck that is roasted and served with a bigarade sauce. When crafted by an experienced chef, it is neither fatty nor dry. The marriage of sweet and sour, crisp and moist is seldom found in any other dish.

For dessert, I will always choose a Crème brûlée. Originating in France, this rich custard based dessert is topped with a layer of caramelized sugar. It's usually served right from the fridge, which leaves it a bit too chilled for my taste. Although the classic preparation relies on the heat from the caramelizing process to warm the custard, I prefer it warm throughout. Most Crème brûlée's are flavored with vanilla, but you can find a variety of variations and flavorings throughout the world.

To top off this great meal, I often enjoy a full bodied, rich tasting Italian wine such as a Montepulciano d'Abruzzo or Amarone della Valpolicella.

If you can find all three of these wonderful offerings at one location and at one sitting, in my opinion, you have found dining nirvana.

What kind of customers do waitstaff like the most?

Waitstaff love serving customers that engage with them. Customers that show their appreciation for the service and food not only through the tip but also through conversation are always a servers favorite customers. The worst customer is one who literally ignores the server. Servers are people and ALL people, not only servers, like to be acknowledged for the service they provide

Are you a bad tipper? Why?

Having been in the restaurant industry for over 20 years, I appreciate all the work that goes into being a server in this industry. Servers are highly underrated and often overlooked in a guests dining experience.

Yes, servers in most chain restaurants are basically food delivery persons.

Although that may sound simplistic at its core, it still involves an enormous amount of stamina to keep up with most chain restaurants mantras to "get em in and get em out". Although most servers in chains are working as servers "until" (until they get s "real" job), they deserve to be rewarded fairly for the service they provide. I guarantee they work harder than most of the guests they serve.

For those of you who belittle the trade, I suggest you try a true fine dining restaurant. Servers at these establishments are trained professionals who view their trade as a career.

Becoming a professional server at a fine dining establishment does not happen by chance. It is a profession that is learned through observation, patience and dedication to better ones craft.

Professional serving is not simply about food delivery. A professional server must of course be in top physical shape to keep up with the demands of the position but must also be a knowledgeable foodie, a caring babysitter, a psychiatrist, a mood setter and an actor.

They must be able to quickly ascertain specifically what each individual guest is looking to get out of their dining experience, who is the alpha, beta at each table, is this a date, business meeting, interview, family get together, do the guests want to be catered to, left alone or somewhere in between. Will the server be acting as a quasi date, mother/father, friend or should they remain unseen.

Servers also need to adjust their personalities to the kitchen staff to assure they receive the attention to detail and timeliness they require. Chefs and their staff can often be prima donna's that require their own "personality management" by the server.

And then after all that effort, there is always the unknowing guest who stiff's the server because they are cheap, think tipping is overrated, unneeded, or because service was slow NOT because of anything the server did but because of inadequacies in the kitchen.

Watch how your server works, see how they interact with not only your table but with others. If they are professionals, they will be a symphony in motion playing tunes to match each persons ears. It is truly a challenging profession that can be both financially and emotionally rewarding.

And then make sure you tip accordingly, for it is oftentimes the server that makes your meal an experience.

Do automated services such as self-checkout machines in grocery stores and self-service kiosks in fast food restaurants kill jobs?

Having read all the yes/no answers regarding this question it's surprising that most have not gotten to the core question which provides the obvious answer to your question.

The first two questions below are NOT that key question I mentioned above (bear with me here).

Do most customers PREFER automated checkouts? If you compare the lines at both, you'll quickly come to an overwhelming conclusion, "NO".

Does automated equipment cost a company great sums of money to buy and maintain? The answer is yes.

Now HERE'S that key question...

So why would a company invest in costly equipment that doesn't increase the customers satisfaction??? Companies NEVER spend money for NO return!

The answer: Companies are doing this because, in the long run, it will save the company money by "eliminating Jobs".

Oh some people might be able to retrain for other jobs in other fields BUT, don't let anyone kid you, automation may help make a company more efficient BUT, automation is primarily focused on reducing a company's dependence on labor to perform a task.

Are restaurant workers at high-end restaurants occasionally allowed to eat the pricey foods as part of their work benefits?

Although it varies with the restaurant, high-end restaurants usually give their employees unlimited access to all their dishes at cost or access to select dishes for free. Drinks such as coffee and iced tea are usually free. In addition, many high-end restaurants give family discounts to the families of all employees.

Whenever a new dish is offered, most high-end restaurants provide all servers with a tasting. At these tastings, the dish will be discussed by the owner or head chef, highlighting what goes into the dish, why it's special and key areas of the dish that the servers should point out when discussing the dish with their guests. This is a valuable tool for the restaurant because, it not only educates the servers on the story behind the dish but also allows them to speak honestly on a dish they have actually enjoyed.

Why "WOULD" anyone start their own restaurant?

The most common answer you'll hear is that they started because of their love of food.

Not necessarily the eating of food (although that is an integral part of it) but the "crafting" of food and subsequent reaction of those who enjoy what they have created.

Basically, people who "would" open restaurants will tell you they love to cook and experiment with new dishes. But a big part of that process includes the reactions they get from family and friends when they serve their dishes. They see themselves as artists and love the creative nature and positive feedback they get from their creations.

You must think of cooking as a creative craft much as a painter would paint a picture. You decide upon what your are going to make (scene to paint), put together your ingredients (paint colors), gather your tools (brushes) and create your dish (paint your painting), all so that you can enjoy the reaction people have to your creation sitting in front of them on their table (hanging on the wall). To chefs, crafting a fine dish IS a work of art!

Why "SHOULD" someone open a restaurant includes part of the "WOULD" answer but should include much more.

You should of course love to cook and experiment with new dishes BUT, you must possess several additional personal characteristics in order to be successful.

You must be able to multitask, understand a balance sheet and P&L, and be able to handle multiple employee and guest personalities, In addition, you must understand how to maintain your supply chain, which includes negotiating with vendors, ordering the correct amount of food stuffs (order too much and you create waste and lose money, order two little and you lose business, create bad will with guests and lose money) and be knowledgeable in branding and advertising. And finally, you must be willing to work abnormally long hours and be on your feet during all that time.

Now that doesn't sound like a great career BUT, so many people have made a success out of it because there is nothing quite like the reward one gets when they can make one person's night an experience they will talk about for a lifetime.

What are some of the best healthy foods to give your kids that will make them think it's their typical junk food?

If you live in the USA, here's the best way to trick your kids into eating healthy. I'm going to suggest a couple of dishes that are completely healthy and dishes that your kids will love. But first you must be willing to use a bit of trickery. If you're in, read on...

There are a few great new products that just came on the market that you can offer your kids. They will be great substitutes for burgers and fries. The great part, if you don't tell them, your kids will never know.

Check out The Impossible Burger and the Beyond Burger for their burgers. Both are made entirely of vegetables BUT, they are NOT your typical veggie burgers. These are burgers for meat eaters. You make them rare, medium rare, well done, just like burgers. They taste just like burgers.

We began offering samples of the Impossible Burgers as sliders at our Crumbzz bistro in Forney, Texas (you can see pictures of them on our website if you want to check them out). Understand that Texas is a "MEAT" state and its not easy switching meat eaters to veggies!

We didn't tell any of our subjects that what they were actually eating was not meat but vegetables. Every one of them loved them and until we told them the actual composition of what they had just eaten, all thought they had just eaten meat. All agreed that they would choose these "burgers" if we put them on our menu. Since then, we have been offering them on our regular menu with great success.

The Beyond Burger, makes vegetable based burgers as well but, they also make sausages that taste just like the real thing! If you're looking for a bratwurst and sweet Italian sausage substitutes, Beyond Burger sausages are for you.

Now on to the fries. All kids like tater tots and I know a few that I think your kids will like. Both are made by Green Giant. One is made from Cauliflower, the other from Broccoli. They look and taste like tater tots, especially the cauliflower ones. Serve them with catchup and you're golden.

By the way, you can also make great "mashed potatoes" with cauliflower. Serve with gravy and they'll never know.

Why do people eat at really bland chain restaurants like Denny's, Village Inn, Applebee's and Olive Garden when independent restaurants are available?

Price and speed. Because much of the food at chains is made in a central commissary (usually owned by the chain) and then shipped to each restaurant to "heat up" think of chains as food preparers not food creators.

In the USA, dining is all about speed and size. Bigger dishes served at an ever faster pace is the American way.

Because of the pressure to produce food quickly, very few chains prepare food from scratch. In addition, because the low-end of the restaurant industry (fast food including most chains) is so price conscious and consumers on the low-end wan't gargantuan portions at cheap prices, chains must "mass-produce their food. Whether this "reality" is caused by the chains themselves or the chains are simply serving a consumer demand, is up for debate.

Many mom and pop places use pre-made dishes that are the same dishes served by the chains especially appetizers and desserts. Gone are the days when a restaurant makes its own unique appetizers and in most chains and mom and pop establishments, the pastry chef is a distant memory. Most appetizers and desserts are purchased from giant distributors like Ben E Keith, Sysco and US Food, kept frozen and heated up on demand.

The difference between mom and pop restaurants and chains can be explained in one word... "consistency". Once you get above ten units (restaurants) you actually leave the restaurant business and enter the "consistency" business.

You don't go to McDonalds for the best burger, you go there because you know, whether it be New York or San Diego, what you get will always be the same. The same holds true for most chains. They are now in the consistency business. They DON'T want a chef at one of their restaurants to prepare their dish differently than the chef at another. Commissary preparation from one central location solves that issue.

Mom and pops try to be different or at least better. Unfortunately, the pressure to deliver big amounts of food at low prices forces them to buy the cheapest pre-made foods or they lose all their price conscious customers.

You won't find that at fine dining restaurants. And, that is why I only operate high-end fine dining restaurants. I want my food to be unique and found no where else.

At fine dining restaurants you make everything from scratch. In our case, we even take it one step further and have NO pre-made dishes (to speed up service, almost every restaurant including many but not all fine dining restaurants pre-make a large amount of their dishes).

What exactly does pre-make mean? A great example of the use of pre-made's is oatmeal. Many breakfast and lunch restaurants will offer oatmeal for breakfast. They make a big pot of that oatmeal on Monday's and pull that pot out each morning. When you order your oatmeal, they scoop out a cup, place it in the microwave and viola, you have your oatmeal in 2–3 minutes. They'll use that method or keep their food in steam-wells which keeps their dishes perpetually hot and ready to serve.

Making it from scratch involves placing the oatmeal in a pot, adding milk and cooking the oatmeal until it reaches the proper consistency. That takes 16 minutes! Nowadays, that's way to long for the average blow-and-go American consumer.

Ever go into a restaurant and be told "sorry no breakfast after 11am or no lunch before 11am"? Know why? That's because restaurants place all their pre- made dishes in the back refrigerators. In the mornings they bring up all their breakfast pre-made's and at 11am they switch out their breakfast pre-mades with their lunch pre-made's. They don't want to pull out a dish for you from the back so, they "STOP" serving at the time they make the switch!

Remember those criticisms I mentioned previously about it taking too long in our Bistro? ~~They~~ Those types of complaints would never happen anywhere else in the world, where dining is a social event that takes hours and consumers "expect" fresh, made from scratch food that, they know will take time to prepare.

If you want fresh made from scratch food, you're going to have to pay the price (making food from scratch involves "actual" chefs, pastry chefs and a larger staff, it involves procuring fresh ingredients that "always"cost more AND involves time, the restaurants and yours. THAT is the price you'll pay to get healthy, fresh and unique dishes. THAT is why people often complain that eating healthy is often so expensive. It is but, your return on your investment in time and money is worth it!

Take some time, don't rush through your meal. Enjoy your food as a social event spent with family and friends. You'll be better for it mentally AND physically!

Is tipping at restaurants an obligation?

This gets into another issue that usually comes up when tipping is discussed and that is the common misconception that tipping simply subsidizes the owners. On the surface this reasoning makes sense. You the customer, through your tipping, make up the difference the restaurant pays its servers. This allows those greedy restaurant owners to reap the benefits. Seems simple on the surface but, as we all know, what often seems simple on the surface, is not always the case. When one takes a deeper dive into this issue, we find that tipping is actually subsidizing the customer! Here's why. If a new minimum wage were mandated tomorrow, all restaurants would do like all other companies do and simply pass those added expenses on to the customer by raising the price of our dishes to reflect those new costs. As a restaurant owner, I have no problem paying a full minimum wage or better to my servers, even at the most recent proposed $15. per hour amount. Why don't I? Because my customers would rebel over the new "higher" prices they would have to pay for their "currently subsidized" meals. So the next time you tip, understand the dynamics behind tipping and treat your server fairly.

Why have roughly half the Chinese restaurants in the US closed in the first year of the pandemic?

For two reasons. One is political the other is business. Let's cover the business reason first. Many Chinese restaurants are buffets and because of the nature of buffets (food sitting out for all to pick at) diners were hesitant to not only share with others but also to congregate as a group. If you look at buffets in general, statistics show that they were hurt the most during the pandemic.

To add insult to injury, politics also came into play. First of all you had the origin of COVID coming from China. Because the nature of how COVID spread was initially unknown, the sharing of food, especially Chinese food was suspect. The fact that former President Trump also tried to link the pandemic to anything Chinese only exacerbated the situation. These two factors were the primary contributors to the damage done to Chinese restaurants.

Are there any fast food restaurants whose food looks the same in reality as in commercials?

I had the challenge of contracting to have my cakes photographed for my website. (www.crumbzz.com) I knew that the quality of the pictures I used would have a direct effect on the sales I made. I soon learned that food photography is a specialized field unto itself that includes part talent and part magic.

Food photographers are specialists in creating the illusion of size, freshness, color and depth. Our photographer had a tool belt that had a set of tools that were designed more for a dentist then a photographer.

Yes, there is some basic food photography knowledge requirements that include:
- Shutter speed, aperture and ISO for creating bright images
- Backlighting
- Side Lighting
- Composition
- Vertical or Horizontal use setup
- Angles

But food photography is less about the equipment you have or even the food your shooting. It's really about what makes food look desirable after sitting under hot photography lights for hours.

It's important to understand what those basics do:
Plating: How you arrange the food
Lighting How you use light to bring out the food's good side
Composition: How you frame the shot
Editing: How to touch-up the photos

Once you understand the basics, you need to learn how to create the magic. The magic is the real trick to understand how to make photographed food look "real".

Food photographers use all kinds of things to "fake" a real look. Most people don't realize that what they're looking at is actually inedible.

Some of the tricks food photographers use include:
- Antacids - that are dropped into soda to create fizz and bubbles
- Shoe polish - which is rubbed onto char-grilled foods to make them shine

- Cardboard - that is placed inside of food such as hamburgers to give them more volume
- Colored waxed - which are melted to look like different sauces
- Cotton balls - which add warmth to a dish. Soaked in water and then microwaved, they are placed behind foods for the look of instant steam
- Dish washing soap - which is mixed into drinks to create surface bubbles
- Fabric protector - which is sprayed onto pancakes to prevent them from absorbing syrup
- Glue - that is used as a replacement for milk for foods like cereal
- Glycerin - which is coated onto seafood to make it look juicier and is mixed with water to make longer-lasting drops
- Hair spray - which is used to make dried-out foods look fresh again
- Incense sticks - that are used to add steam to shots
- Lacquer - which is painted onto rice to make the grains shinier and less sticky
- Lemon extract - which is used to remove the blue letters and numbers printed on food bottles.
- Liquid glucose - which is mixed into noodles to make them look hot and fresh
- Mashed potatoes - which are used as a replacement for ice cream. Photographers use them so they don't have to deal with melting ice cream, can easily change the color to match a desired flavor. Mashed potatoes are also injected into meat to give it volume, and stuffed into a pie to provide picture perfect slices
- Motor oil - which is used to replace dull-looking syrups
- Plastic ice cubes - that don't melt are used to replace real ice cubes that do
- Shaving cream - that is used to replace whipped cream since it's less runny and is easier to shape

- Spray deodorant - which is used to make certain fruits shine
- Toothpicks - which are used to prop up food for better angles and increased volume

So the next time you look at that delicious looking burger and ice cream float photo, you now understand just what goes into making it look so good.

What legal action can I take against a restaurant which is opened just next to my house?

Your beef isn't with the restaurant but with your city, specifically with the codes that allowed that happen. If your house is in or adjacent to a commercial zone that restaurant is entirely within its rights to be there. Did the zoning change from when you purchased your home? We're you notified as described by law? Did the restaurant apply for and receive all the required approvals to locate there? Is the restaurant in compliance with all laws? These are just a few of the rabbit holes you must venture down to arrive at an answer to your question.

What are two (2) menu evaluating factors that can be used to evaluate the success of a menu?

It's actually pretty simple. Positioning is important. Viewers tend to look to the top right corner first, so place your specials there. Continually move the positioning of your menu items on a quarterly basis and track your sales. Visualizing is an important part of human reaction. You don't want to overload your menu with pictures and copy. As always, less is more. It's better to distribute a few professionally created photos of key dishes than to load your menu with a picture of each dish.

Copy is also important. As mentioned, people are motivated by visual cues, copy can also create a visual picture of the dish (e.g. a "16 ounce prime steak, seared to perfection over mesquite coals" sounds much more enticing than "a 16 oz steak made to choice". Paint a picture with each description.

Finally, track your sales. If you have designed your menu properly and rotate as mentioned, tracked sales will tell you which dishes best satisfy your guests needs. Keep your offerings limited. Don't keep adding new dishes, instead, purge those that don't sell and replace with new ones. By doing this, you will have a menu that serves not only your guests but also your restaurant.

Has the Covid 19 pandemic so altered eating out to have a long-term effect on restaurant viability? Should wait staff seriously consider a new profession?

Although there will be quite a few restaurants that will not make it through the pandemic (estimates run as high as 50% + reduction in the independent restaurant base), when the pandemic is over (projections are 6-month's to 1 year), those restaurants that have survived will be in excellent position to flourish. Multiple restaurant industry surveys point to a pent-up demand for people to get out and socialize as they did prior to the pandemic.

What this means to existing wait staff is a mixed bag. On the negative side, since there will be half as many restaurants, there will be half as many job openings. Because of the quantity of available wait staff, restaurants will choose only the best of the best for their wait staff.

On the plus side, all those restaurants who remain in operation after the pandemic has receded, will be busier than ever. In addition, because of the reduction of competition and the need to catch up on lost earnings, prices will be higher (which extrapolates into higher tips for wait staff).

The end result is a common refrain, only the strong will survive in both restaurants and wait staff but, those who do (the best of the best) will reap the rewards.

How do I make a profit easily in a restaurant business?

You don't! The restaurant business is a tough business to enter and maintain. It's expensive to get into, it's margins are tight, it requires a skilled labor pool and because of waste, it's product line is extremely challenging to manage.

So, who would, in their right mind, venture into such a challenging environment?

One doesn't enter into such a challenging business because of the numbers. Most of those who take on the challenge "Love" to cook, "Love" to serve others and "Love" to leave their mark. See a pattern here? Entry into this field serves to satiate an emotional not financial need.

There very few careers that allow a creative person to leave a memory on their guests that can last a lifetime!

What is the biggest no-no in fine dining?

From a servers point of view it's clearing a dish before EVERYONE is finished. This is now become a common occurrence in the United States where everyone is in a hurry and restaurants are intent on "turning tables", but, fine dining etiquette makes it clear that it is impolite to take an individual dish from the table while someone else is still eating

Have any restaurants eliminated or toned down their background music so that so that servers and patrons don't have to yell at one another to be heard (in light of the possibility of spreading the Covid virus)?

In the States, the restaurant profit basis is based on turnover. Years ago, when someone wanted to know how successful your restaurant was, they asked "what is your top line revenue". Nowadays, they ask "how many table turns do you generate a day". Unfortunately, the music they play (often called "metro music" in the industry) is designed with a fast upbeat and to be played at a high volume. This is based on multiple studies that show that music played this way encourages guests to order fast, eat fast and leave quickly. This is found most often in the States and parts of Canada. In the rest of the world, dining is a social event, designed to be enjoyed with friends and families at a much slower pace, often hours at a time.

At my Crumbzz bistro in a suburb of Dallas, Texas, we are intent on matching the old world style of made from scratch dishes, presented at a leisurely pace. Because we feature internationally sourced dishes, our atmosphere is more like the great bistros found in Italy or France than small town Texas. The sounds of Bocelli & Brightman fill our dining area at a volume that allows guests to hear one another speak. We NEVER rush a guest!

It's a choice we made when we opened to offer what today would be considered a "different" dining experience to our guests. We knew early on that we would not be for everyone and would most assuredly take a hit to our bottom line but, following the US style of dining was a price we were not willing to pay.

So, whenever you hear that loud "METRO" music playing in a restaurant, you now know where that restaurants primary focus is placed and it's NOT on you hanging around for a leisurely dining experience.

Do retail workers have the right to refuse service if the customer refuses to wear a mask?

Absolutely. Have you ever seen the signs, "No Shirt, No Shoes, No Service. They have been adorning the windows of restaurants for years. Nowadays you can add "No Mask" to that list. Businesses, (any business) has the right to deny service to anyone they choose for any reason they choose except for a few exceptions. They can't deny service to someone because of their race, color, religion, national origin or disability. In addition, some states and cities, don't permit service denial because of a persons sexual orientation.

We have always been about healthy eating. Accordingly, at my bistro's we require all guests to wear a mask except when eating. If a person chooses not to wear a mask, they have that right. And because of my concern for the safety of my staff and guests, as the business owner, I have the right to deny them service.

As a food service worker, have you ever been asked to serve food that you knew was too old to serve?

As a restauranteur, it's not only morally reprehensible but also clear that the risk reward analysis confirms that it's NEVER worth it. Your gain of a few dishes of food you would have thrown out versus the chance that your guests get sick and you get closed down just doesn't add up.

Do subsequent coronavirus pandemic restaurant closures produce a glut of used restaurant equipment?

As with all things in life, for every loser there is a winner. In this case, the losers are all those restaurants that went out of business during the pandemic. The winners are not only the auction houses who specialize in the sale of used restaurant equipment but also surviving restaurants who need equipment and those who are crazy enough to open a restaurant.

As the laws of supply and demand take hold, the glut of equipment will most assuredly lower prices on all types of restaurant equipment to those willing purchasers.

If I want to open a restaurant, then how can I differentiate it and make it profitable?

You must first start holistically, then you can get into specifics. As with any business, you need to find a need that is not being fulfilled and provide a solution. If you can't find a unique need, then you will need to find a unique solution to an existing need.

How do you position your restaurant, that being the brand you project, is all important. Yes, take out and curb side is big right now but both will fade when the virus recedes. People will want to get out and socialize once again and there will be plenty of room to provide a solution to that requirement. But, to be successful, your solution must be different from all others. Being the best burger restaurant doesn't cut it!

What comes to mind here is a famous quote by the greatest hockey player of all time, Wayne Gretzky. When I asked what made him different from every other hockey player, Gretzky stated *"I skate to where the puck is going not where it has been."*

Don't follow where everyone else has been or is going. Chart a new path that separates you from all others. Do your research, find the need and create the market by leading instead of following in others footsteps.

How do I request a store/restaurant to open in my city?

Send demographics that support sufficient numbers of the type of client the company serves to make it worthwhile to open a location in your community.

No company opens a store without a sound basis confirming enough business to be successful.

J Stephen's Actual To-Do List

This is the actual TO-DO list that J Stephen Sadler kept as he built his cake and bistro business. It's and excellent deep dive into the challenges and time commitments an entrepreneur can be expected to make as they build their business from the ground up. As you read through the list, you will get insights into site location and preparation

LEGAL/FINANCIAL/LICENSING

Call tax adviser regarding funding for bistro buildout
09/02/10
- Called (LB) regarding corporate structure relative to various tax ramification scenarios

09/07/10
- Discussed:
- Crafting Financial for business plan
    - o JSS to do. JSS to send Figures
- Deductions of expenses
    - o Can deduct (depreciate all equip purchases)
    - o Can deduct all cog's
    - o Will get tax credit for appliance purchases
- Discussed setting up Non Profit for environmental, fair trade and sustainable farming donations
    - o Set up Crumbzz International Green Fund
    - o Need to get IRS approval to set up
- Negotiated funding with city for buildout. JSS to provide funding for equipment and all sundries.

PROJECT COMPLETED

Finish Minizz Nutrition Labels
07/6/10
- Found websites that provide nutrition information for recipes and calorie count

07/12/10
- Created labels for Crumbzz Cakes

07/26/10
- Created labels for Minizz

08/28/10
- Found issues with labeling requirements

09/27/10
- Redid labels to fit Minizz and cakes

10/17/10
- Redid label layouts

10/29/10
- Picked up 8 ½" X 11" full sheet white adhesive labels for temporary nutritional labels

11/01/10
- Printed and cut labels for all cakes/Minizz

11/2/10
- Designed permanent nutrition labels for printing

11/2/10
- Ordered permanent nutrition labels
- Designed nutrition labels for printing
- Ordered nutrition labels from (UL)

11/09/10
- Provided final approval on print to (UL)

11/12/10
- Received pre-printed nutrition labels from (UL)

PROJECT COMPLETED

Create non-profit and open bank account

09/08/10
- Called (PS) with (CC) and set up Crumbzz International Green Foundation, Inc. paperwork to follow ($XXX) 09/24/10
- Received required paperwork to open account from (ML) of (P) Bank (direct)
    - Articles of Organization—I need to know the nature of your business.

- Operating Agreement in order to identify any managers, members, or elected officers.
- Proof of the EIN—the letter provided by the IRS
- Identification on all signers. i.e. photo copy of driver's license.
- Registration of Foreign Entity", also called "Certificate of Authority", since your business was formed outside of Texas

10/05/10
- Received Corporate incorporation papers for company

10/07/10
- Called (PS) of (CC)
    - Will correct mailing address error on the Company (shows Millennium)
    - Stated that we don't need "Certificate of Authority" if we open bank account in WY

10/13/10
- Opened acct. Deposited $XXX in acct

PROJECT COMPLETED

Set up Crumbzz & Non Profit bank accounts in Quickbooks

10/20/10
- Purchased Quickbooks

10/21/10
- Completed Vendor info input
- Completed Customer info input

10/22/10
- Completed account setup in Quickbooks

PROJECT COMPLETED

Apply for City of Dallas Food Handlers Certification

12/30/10
- FedEx'd application and check

01/4/11
- Need City of Dallas Certificate
- Go to 7901 Go Forth Road Dallas, TX with copy of

state certificate and DL
- Pay fee $XXX
- Get City of Dallas certificate
- Get back $XX fee

03/16/11
- Pick up and paid for ($XXX) City of Dallas Registered Food Service Manager Certificate for Dallas location

PROJECT COMPLETED

Apply for State of Texas Food Safety License
12/30/10
- Contacted State of TX to inquire on requirements. Told to send fee $XXXX to state. Take course, pass exam, receive certification, take copy to local municipality to get local license
- Paid fee
- Accessed Learn2Serve website.
  - Applied for exam
  - Paid fee ($XXX course and $XX exam)

01/11/11
- Passed course

01/14/11
- Passed exam, received certificate

PROJECT COMPLETED

Purchase Product Barcodes
5/2/14
- Contacted GS1 to purchase a membership to get a barcode prefix. Purchased prefix: KEY MEMBERSHIP INFORMATION EXPLAINED:
  - Key Membership Information: (1) Company Name: XXXXXXXX; Account Number: XXXXXX; Username: XXXXX; Password: XXXXXX; Your GS1 Company Prefix Certificate and license agreement are attached.; Our Prefix allows us to create 10 U.P.C. barcodes and 10 locations. JSS accessed the

Gs1 Data Driver website: XXXXX and created barcodes for all Crumbzz Consumer Retail Products: (1) Crumbzz Chocolat de la Terre 10" Crumb Cake; (2) Crumbzz Ruby Red Raspberry 10" Crumb Cake; (3) Crumbzz Old World Cinnamon Streusel 10" Crumb Cake; (4) Crumbzz Caramel Seal Salt 10" Crumb Cake; (5) Crumbzz Liege Waffles; (6) Crumbzz Minizz Snack Cake Trio Assortment; (7) Crumbzz Vanilla Cinnamon Crumbler Ice Cream; (8) Crumbzz Chocolate Caramel Sea Salt Ice Cream

PROJECT COMPLETED

Get guidance on legality of offering the rights to open a Crumbzz location as a reward for the Crumbzz Crowd funding reward for funding program

05/23/14
- Emailed (ML) regarding legality of offering.
    1. naming rights versus
    2. biz op offerings versus
    3. franchise options

05/27/14
- Received a call from (ML) regarding crowd funding. JSS provided a brief overview. (ML) would like to meet to discuss further. Will charge $XXXX to review our program's legality and compliance with the crowd funding site(s) requirements. Will provide guidance on a going forward plan. Set up meeting. At this meeting, I will need to know
    1) plan of how to use the money to help your business,
    2) a rough budget of what is needed to achieve your base goal,
    3) proposed incentives and estimated costs, and
    4) a list promotional graphics and any products you are planning on using in promoting your crowdfunding.

06/23/14
- Met with (ML) discussed potential legal challenges with crowdfunding program as structured.
- Due to potential legal issues, decided to shelve project at this time.

PROJECT COMPLETED

Create Crumbzz Business Plan for Financing
05/28/14
- Updated Crumbzz original business plan adding 2011/2012/2013 Financials. Adjusted plan to reflect European Bistro's and Tasting Pavilion's.
- Need to add a 5-year plan and a buy out plan. JSS to craft.

06/03/14
- JSS crafted and presented 5-year plan and a buy out plan to attorney

PROJECT COMPLETED

Create a Crumbzz Cash Flow Analysis
06/01/14
- Updated Crumbzz original cash flow analysis for 2014 2011/2012/2013 (previously completed). Adjust plan to reflect projected European Bistro's and Tasting Pavilion's.

PROJECT COMPLETED

Create a Crumbzz P&L Analysis
06/05/14
- Updated Crumbzz original P&L analysis for 2014 2011/2012/2013 (previously completed). Adjust plan to reflect projected European Bistro's and Tasting Pavilion's.

PROJECT COMPLETED

Become a member of Forney Historic league. (Legal requirement under contract with City of Forney).

06/03/14
- Signed up as corporate member

PROJECT COMPLETED

VENDOR PROCUREMENT

Get ingredients together for trip to demo cakes at Callebaut Chocolate's corporate offices - (include camera)

08/23/10
- Printed recipes
- Packed and shipped case

09/02/10
- Visited with Callebaut team in Chicago. Crafted 12 cakes in front of team. Used several different types of chocolate.

09/03/10
- Team tasted and rated cakes

09/05/10
- Re-tasted cakes. Ratings changed. Team to review why change

09/06/10
- Flew back to Dallas

09/17/10
- Got results why ratings changed. Picked chocolate to be used for Choc. de la Terre cakes. Placed initial order.

PROJECT COMPLETED

Open food distributor acct at (JB)

10/01/10
- Spoke with XX at (JB). Will send out app., price list and catalog. Start Amex go to acct billing
- Received app
- Sent in app and all requested paperwork, licenses

11/12/10
- Met with XXXX. Received samples of fruit toppings

and flour. Discussed pricing (too high) told him (BK) was lower. Will work on it and see what he can do.

11/28/10
- Emailed XXX requested updated pricing as previously requested

11/30/10
- Opened account

PROJECT COMPLETED

Open Account at (BEK)

10/07/10
- Requested (BEK) contact info from (SVM)

10/08/10
- LM for (SVM) on cell
- Spoke with (SVM) Asked for contact at (BEK)
- Received contact info for (BEK)

10/12/10
- Called (RF) at (BEK) LM
- (RF) called. Will send app and price list. JSS to send product requirements
- Sent product requirements

10/15/10
- Sent fully executed application in to (RF)

10/18/10
- Received pricing from (RF) Do not carry Vanilla or Callebaut 75%. Will get Callebaut if we need it.

11/03/10
- Asked (RK) if account has been activated
- Received reply, acct opened, account # XXXXX
- Provided business incorporation date XXXX.

PROJECT COMPLETED

Open FedEx, UPS & USPS Accounts & Order pre-printed shipping labels from UPS and FedEx

10/21/10
- Called FedEx to order thermal printer. Awaiting rep call back to process (acct # XXXXXXX)

10/22/10
- Spoke w/ FedEx rep. Will have acct rep call JSS ASAP
- Called UPS to order labels. Need to re-open old existing acct. Will have a rep call JSS by 10/26

10/26/10
- Called UPS and FedEx regarding activating accounts
- Received call from FedEx,(KS) (Acct Mgr) for Fed Ex
  - Provided her w/ (CB) contact info. to assimilate Fed Ex into our website.
  - Will put together program for Crumbzz and contact JSS to discuss package
  - Will bring packages to Fed Ex until scheduled pick up is set up

10/29/10
- Received contract from FedEx
- FedEx Labels on the way

11/02/10
- FedEx Labels arrived

11/09/10
- Obtained prices under new contract for input on client ordering form
- Spoke to (KD) re: link to order on Crumbzz website.
- Provided link XXXXXXXXXXXXX
- Sent link and contact info. to (CB) for insertion in Crumbzz website

11/08/10
- Activated online service. Sent test package (FedEx)

11/09/10
- Test package received. System approved & signed off.

PROJECT COMPLETED

Finalize design & selection of t-shirt vendor and place order

08/23/10
- Called (LM) re: pricing. Also mentioned that gun shirt still not right

08/25/10
- Received pricing from (LM)

09/08/10
- Spoke w/ (LM) set appt for 09/09/10
- Called (B) at logo company. Provided drawings plus new CrumbzzNatic's Like The Top shirt. Will have bid 09/08/10

09/09/10
- Met w/ (LM) to review shirts

09/10/10
- Met with (ON) Will have samples on 09/18/10 Received pricing from (BM) at Logo company for rhinestone and glitter t-shirts

09/19/10
- Met with (ON). Reviewed samples. Approved woman's v-neck shirt. (ON) to provide samples and pricing on woman's v-neck and tunic and men's t-shirt on 09/21/10

09/24/10
- Called XXXXXXX (they supply Tyler's w/ shirts) spoke w/(M). Provided her with sample designs. She will be sending samples of shirts and design suggestions next week (incl. glitter) men's & ladies shirts. Woman's-Designer shirt- "Spatula", Knock-around Shirt-"Hand over the cake"; Men's-Designer shirt -will create Knock- around Shirt-"Dbl ZZ Me."

09/30/10
- Found shirt/design I liked. Asked store owner to have creator call (LC) t-shirt designer contacted JSS. Discussed JSS ideas. Limited 24 pc runs 2 styles each for men and women. Specific Crumbzz "Look" for each. Set 10/08/10 meeting to review ideas.

10/08/10
- Reviewed t-shirt plan; 1 designer shirt each M&W black; Spatula women; Small ZZ men; 1 knock around shirt each M & W white or other color; Dbl ZZ Me men; No one gets hurt women; 1 either CrumbzzNatic, Caker or Good Enough To Be Crumbzz giveaway shirts. All shirts to be organic. 24 shirts per (limited edition). (LC) to get back w/designs/ideas, etc during the week. JSS to send eps file. (LC) to sign each shirt on bottom left. Shirts to be one of a kind unique designs. Meet next Friday to review. JSS sent eps file

10/12/10
- Received first passes at designs from (LM). Replied that designs were too basic. Will work up more detailed designs

10/13/10
- Reviewed new designs from (LC). Good. Requested some suggested changes. Decided on ; 1 black designer shirt for M/W each ($XX retail); 1 white knock around shirt for M/W each ($XX retail); 1 give away shirt ($? Inexpensive). (LC) to get back w/ new designs and prices
on 10/15/10

10/15/10
- Met w/ (LC). JSS will order shirts directly from t-shirt vendor
  - Approved "Good Enough To Be Crumbzz" shirt as giveaway shirt. (LC) to do the following: Rework spatula shirt (JSS drew out what it should look like); Rework gun shirt (JSS sent drawing of what is needed); Make ZZ in men's designer shirt smaller
- JSS placed order for giveaway "Good Enough To Be Crumbzz" t- shirts with (CT) tee-shirt company. Had shirts shipped to (LC) to have printed. Specifics on shirt order: Anvil Heavyweight 100% 6.1 Cotton T-Shirt #979; Charcoal Grey; XXX shirts (XXX each

S/M/L); $XX per shirt - Total $XXX; Free shipping/ no tax ; 24 hrs to process 3-4 days shipping. Specifics on printing: 2 color front/one color sleeve $XXX $XX per shirt. Specifics on art work; $XXX for XX t-shirts ($XX shirt + $XX printing + $XX art work = $XX per shirt
- Applied for a wholesale account @(AA)
- Applied for a wholesale account @ (F)

10/20/10
- Reviewed drawings with (LC). Will have Final (amended) drawings on ladies and men's fashion t's, ladies gun and men's dbl ZZ me Knock-a-round's by 10/21/10. Paid deposit for give away shirt to commence production of shirt

10/21/10
- Applied for account with (AA)

10/22/10
- Approved giveaway shirt design. Paid Deposit to (LC). Sent request to woman focus group on spatula shirt. Ask to choose center or bottom. Approved ZZ shirt w/ changes
- Emailed executed wholesale acnt application @ (AA)
- Met w/(LC). Reviewed shirt, don't like color "Storm Grey"
- Contacted (CT) tee-shirts Received an RA number and UPS shipping label for return.
- Ordered "Charcoal" shirts. Will arrive @ (LC) on 10/26/10

10/23/09
- Focus group results show a 2 to 1 favoring the bottom graphic
- Returned "Storm Grey" shirts to vendor

10/25/10
- Corrected shirts (charcoal) arrived. (LC) will take to printer

11/01/10
- Visited Tyler's Shirts to see (AA) shirts. Copied down

item numbers on potential shirts
- Called (AA). Account not yet active. Got account up and running. Picked, ordered and paid for all remaining shirts
- Asked for update from (LC) re: "Good enough to be Crumbzz" t- shirt status. Designers still not available. Asked him to continue to ping them

11/04/10
- T-shirts arrived from (AA) included; XXXX women's knock- around; XXXX men's knock-around; XXXX men's designer; XXXX women's designer med, lg. received, sm.
  back ordered

11/05/10
- Changed color on woman's t-shirt to see how it would look as a black t-shirt w/grey design. Looks good. Also, filled in spatula in grey (lost it when it was black) and changed scrolling to black as it goes over spatula. Sent updated design to (LC) asked him to re-do with my changes
- Met w/(LC). Picked up completed "Good enough to be Crumbzz" t-shirts. Provided (to go to print): XXXX men's designer ZZ shirts. Paid balance due $XX for "Good Enough To Be Crumbzz t-shirts and $XX deposit on ZZ shirts Total $XXX

11/08/10
- Received printer address and designs, signed off on both designs
- IM'D Dallas Art Institute for an artist who can draw the two remaining t-shirts Gun and Dbl ZZ Me
- Called(AA), asked about status of backordered t-shirts. Girl said it shows order was available to ship on 11/3/10. Will check & call JSS with what she finds out

11/10/10
- Received email from (AF) of (AA) "delay." Informed (LC) of delay. Will bring all shirts at once

11/13/10

- Contacted (BAW) regarding t-shirt production pricing was $XX + shipping per shirt ($XX per shirt inclusive.) Will call back if I decide to order

11/15/10
- Contacted (BM) of (LD) Logo Company, requested updated pricing. Received pricing from (LD). Created Pricing comparison chart
- Contacted (DTS) (S) for pricing. Provided two shirt designs Dbl ZZ and Gun for artwork pricing. Received cost to print $xxx per shirt, await design cost
- Contacted (MG) Tees. Provided spec's on Gun and Dbl ZZ t- shirts requested price on art design and printing
- Contacted(ID); Spoke w/ (M). Transferred to (KR) (corp accts). Opened corporate acct (sent credit app). Agreed on a price of $XX per shirt, all in. Went to (ID) to view designs. Discussed design specifics with (KR) Picked up samples of silver. Requested status update on sales order XXXXXXX backordered item #XXXX in Black size Small, qty 12 from (AA)(AF) Due in

11/16/10. Items will be
   shipped today ETA 11/18/10
- Asked (LC) to send eps files of artwork for ladies spatula and men's ZZ designer shirts. Will send tonight
- Sent PO email approval on printing all four remaining shirts to (KR) at I(ID) 11/18/10.
- Received back ordered t-shirts from (AA)

11/19/10
- Delivered all t-shirts to (ID) for printing

11/22/10
- Approved final designs for all t-shirts. Provided approval to print

11/29/09
- Received last open design (Spatula Gun from (ID). Asked to reduce size of spatula and match Crumbzz spatula and slim/ elongate fingers and nails of hand

12/02/10
- Sent approval on final design to (ID)

PROJECT COMPLETED

Complete vendor/product selection of wax seal and place initial order

06/23/10
- Cut deal with (NI)
- Opened up corporate account

07/06/10
- Received sample seal and wax (not acceptable)

09/17/10
- Spoke with (D) at (WS) in Poland for wax seals. Product looks good. Sent logo sample. (D) to send samples (two colors red- burgundy) on 09/22/10. 25% disc. Will work with Webmaster to link order pages. Will bid a 2" rd, sq, rect. Peel & Stick and wax

09/21/10
- Received samples and pricing

09/23/10
- Received samples wax and wax gun to test. Tested seals, decided to use pre-made peal and stick seals (needs higher and deeper Crumbzz logo then provided

09/27/10
- Called (D) want larger seal with deeper logo (similar to Grand Marnier bottle. (D) stated that the Grand Marnier process is a different process. Could get close to what they are doing. JSS requested a 2 1/4" w X 1 3/4" h red seal. Lip must be higher than peal and stick samples provided and logo must be wider and deeper than the Crumbzz stamp provided. (D) explained that to get deeper and wider will need a certain font only. Could be a problem with the logo's provided by clients. Discussed several different design options for Crumbzz logo. (D) will get her designer to produce drawings now. May have sample drawings today. Will offer clients two choices. If they use their logo (with their type) will be shallow. If they use our type will be

deeper. Will let client choose
- Received sample Crumbzz logos

09/28/10
- Spoke w/(D). Seal needs to be much thicker and bleed must be at least 3/8" thick . Seal should consist of two circles. Glue patch must be wider than ribbon (ribbon is 3/4") to allow wax seal to stick to box.
- Requested a sample drawing of a round and oval seal each with two designs: Inner circle design 1- the letter "C" ; Inner circle design 2-"Spatula from logo" ; "C" font in inner circle to be "Deloise"; Outer circle design for all types; Top-Simply Natural; Bottom-World's Finest; Font and placement/size for outer circle to match Beverly Hills font (wine co. sample provided by (D)). (D) will have her designer create art work for the above ASA

09/29/10
- Received updated drawings. Chose 3 to test. Negotiated price for 3 seals ($XXX each + shipping) will have by 09/30/10

09/30/10
- Received sample wax seals. Too big/ look fake

10/04/10
- Spoke w/ (D) about problem. Will work with team to see what they can do o 10/04/10
- Contacted (TS) Wax Seals (UK) regarding their real wax seals. Requested pricing, and processing time

10/05/10
- Received email from (M) OF (TS) 6-8 weeks processing time. Asked what our quantity requirements were. Provided overview of Crumbzz w/ quantity and timeline requirements

10/06/10
- Received email from (M) processing 1-2 weeks price $XXp sterling (approx. $XXUSD) XX% payment at order, bal prior to dispatch. Crumbzz pays for shipping

- Provided (WSC) current price list to (TS) Asked if they could match price. Asked for samples w/ Crumbzz log (Provided logo) Crumbzz to pay shipping
- Received email from (D) (WS). Suggested use wax different color (can make to order). Will send wax and seals (regular post)

10/07/10
- Asked for samples w/Crumbzz logo ASAP

10/08/10
- Received sample wax from (WSC) ((D)) no seals.

10/12/10
- Asked for ETA on shipped samples. Reply 10-14 days

10/15/10
- Requested seals from (WSC).com

11/10/10
- Alerted (TS) that we still haven't received seal.

11/14/10
- Received address from (TS) from (MC); "The address for the wax seals despatch is: XXXXXXXX"
- Sent (KS of FedEx email requesting pricing on shipping from Poland

11/15/10
- Received cost estimate to ship seals $ XXXX 2-4 days

11/22/10
- Tried melting wax to create our own seal. Not acceptable. Environmentally unfriendly.

11/24/10
- Sent email to (M) "(M)- Still no seals. 11/26/10
- Received reply, declined to make seals

11/29/10
- Received seals from (TS)
- Spoke to (DT) at (WSC). in Vancouver, CA. Can she match seals from (TS) seals If yes will purchase.
- Scanned seals for (DT) review. Would like to see actual seals.
- Overnighted seals to (DT) for review

12/01/10
- Spoke w/(DT), confident they can match seals. Informed her we want the 1 1⁄2" round seal (as provided in sample wax seals) w/the Crumbzz logo Simply Natural and Worlds Finest in border. Will call JSS w/ confirmation of capability by 12/3/10

12/06/10
- Called (DT) at (WSC), asked status. Was waiting on JSS choice. JSS chose spatula. Will get back today w/ price and ability. Told her need within 1-week. (DT) will have ready by Tuesday of next week. Spatula w/ striped background. Can discuss required format

12/07/10
- Received invoice for seals (PayPal) as well as summary of agreement: "We will produce 1.5" round wax seals and ship via FedEx Ground for $XX per seal. All seals will be produced in Dark Red with the perm. adh on the back. If the client wishes to expedite, the additional cost for orders under 500 pieces is 2 day service is $XX or Overnight is $XX $XX. As discussed, please have your webmaster contact (M). He manages our website and can be reached at XXXXX or at XXXXXXX

12/08/10
- Paid invoice: Amount: $XXX USD, Transaction Date: December 8, 2010, Transaction ID: XXXXXXX

12/09/10
- Sent email to (DT) adding one additional element we agreed to in our conversation (verbal agreement) "as agreed, std ground shipping will be free of charge (paid for by WSC)."
- Seals shipped
- Received email agreeing to JSS addition to agreement.

12/11/10
- Received wax seals

PROJECT COMPLETED

Open Crumbzz hosting and email accounts with Go Daddy
12/03/09
- Registered crumbzz.com with Go Daddy

07/22/10
- Purchased hosting account from Go Daddy

08/30/10
- Purchased SSL Certificate from Go Daddy

10/20/10
- Registered crumbzz.net with Go Daddy (Forwarded to crumbzz.com)

11/10/10
- Registered jstephen @ crumbzz.com; greatcakes @ crumbzz.com; accounting @ crumbzz.com

01/16/11
- Extended all Crumbzz url's (except crumbzz.net) to 2013

02/17/11
- Registerd clientservice @ crumbzz.com
- Extended crumbzz.net to 2013

PROJECT COMPLETED

Select tea/coffee provider
08/23/10
- Called (CC) (spoke to S) not back from holiday until 09/01/10. Spoke w/ (R) (@ (SG)) suggested (CC) use Minizz box create tea/coffee/insert pkgs. to fit in Minizz holes

09/07/10
- Called and set up 09/08/10 – 10:30 am meeting

09/08/10
- Met w/ Boys, agreed on pricing. Called (R) from (SG). Will work with (P) on packaging for cross sell program that will compliment the Crumbzz packaging and fit into the Minizz boxes
- JSS will sell them the Minizz boxes for their use (cost +10%)

09/16/10
- Picked up sample bags from (SG), Not acceptable. Need to find packaging

09/20/10
- JSS found packaging (NW catalog). Called (CC) to set up meeting to review. Ordered samples from (NW) (due in 7-10 days)

09/23/10
- Received samples from (NW). Not acceptable. Told (P) needs to find something acceptable ASAP

09/27/10
- Received gift box from (NW). Looks good

09/28/10
- Dropped off sample box to (CC)

10/06/10
- Requested pricing on product from (K)

10/19/10
- Spoke to (P) Wants to use their own box packaging for cross-sell pgm. (JSS to view when next by store). Will send out pricing by weeks end JSS to get XX% discount off retail

10/20/10
- Received pricing on tea/coffee from (CC)

11/10/10
- Sent updated order form and price list to (CC)

12/02/10
- Called LM for (JF) of (KD). Want to discuss pricing (coffee/tea) and gift packaging

02/17/11
- Called (JF) of (KD). Want to discuss pricing (coffee/tea) and gift packaging. Will open account for Crumbzz and provide a Customer # and Password on 02/21/11. Will call JSS at that time. Will also research specialists in tea and coffee to see if we can set up a tasting to match products. At worst, will send samples for Crumbzz to test.

02/21/11
- (CC) moving from location. Not sure where and when to re-open.

02/21/11
- Contacted (GE) regarding tea and coffee supply

02/24/11
- Performed tasting at (GE)

03/10/11
- Focus group tasting on coffees and teas. Picked; TEAS - Red Rooibos, English breakfast, pomegranate, and secha green; COFFEES - TX pecan, medium Colombian, dark French and decaf. ESPRESSO'S - Lavazza blue and decaf.

03/12/11
- Decided to go with (GE). Signed contract. placed first order. Order to include espresso machine. JSS owns all other coffee equipment.

PROJECT COMPLETED

Get Smart Phone app up and running

09/21/10
- Spoke with (CB) webmaster regarding building Smart Phone app. Scheduled phone meeting for 09/23/10

09/24/10
- Spoke with (CB). Discussed Smart Phone app. Focus on ordering and voting. Will brainstorm iPhone app. And come back w/some ideas.

09/29/10
- Asked for update. No work done. Had issue with purchasing using web link. Don't want to use web link. Will research further

10/07/10
- IM'd (CB). Asked for update on progress. Figuring out the best interface to separate the seasonal stuff that will need to be downloaded from the site and the stuff that is constant. Asked for ETA. Told, not sure...

10/08/10

- Asked for estimate $ to build Smart Phone app

11/02/10
- Provided (CB) with Authorize.net requirements for iPhone app's

11/06/10
- Decided on holding off on smart phone app.

PROJECT COMPLETED

Contract with a retail baker to handle baking requirements for Retail Consumer Packaging (RCP)

09/03/13
- Received introduction email from (RDV) with (TW) of XX Processors

12/11/13
- Signed NDA with XX

1/15/14
- Techmar/Crumbzz Recipe/Processes for pricing

1/30/14
- Received volume query from XX. JSS provided projections

02/07/14
- Received pricing on cakes. Price does not include any packaging or freight." Cake pricing varied by Nlavor because of different cost basis. Pricing was not acceptable.

05/2/14
- Sent (TW) the following email: (TW)-. Asked for a re-price based on our cost to produce the individual 10" round cakes

05/12/14
- Received updated pricing from (TW): "After reviewing the current costing here is an update on the selling price.
- The pricing includes the bake in mold, additional packaging be added on after it has been determined.
  - Cinnamon Streusel $XXXX
  - Chocolate $XXXX

- Fruit $XXXX
- Caramel $XXXX
- Decided to utilize this company when bulk production is required.

PROJECT COMPLETED

Contract with an ice cream producer for Crumbzz Consumer Products Division (retail sales) Cinnamon Streusel Crumbler and Chocolate Caramel Sea Salt ice creams

10/3/13
- Called XXXXX ice cream (Crumbzz current provider) to discuss possibility of private labeling Crumbzz ice cream. Don't private label, only produce in 3-gal containers.

10/05/13
- Visited (H) of (WAH) Custard discussed them producing our ice cream to our spec's.

10/23/13
- Sent (H) NDA. Met with (A) (H) Mgr.) to discuss pricing and tests o 11/1/13
- Performed test on (H) ice cream. Test not a success. Not up to quality required.

11/21/13
- Performed second testing JSS specifications. Test passed.

12/10/13
- Created cost analysis: They provide no packaging or labels for this product. Based on our discussions, Crumbzz will provide the streusel and crumbs and the pint packaging. (WAH) ice cream currently sells for $XXX sells it for $XXX (8 pints - $XXX per pint) to Central Market. (WAH) sells their pints (retail) in their store for $XXX.

01/12/14
- Performed test on second flavor on (WAH) ice cream,

test not successful. Quality not up to Crumbzz standards

02/24/14
- Performed another test on (WAH) ice cream, test not successful. Although quality back up to our spec's, because they spoon their ice cream into the containers, not able to achieve the ribbon of streusel/crumbs we want

04/12/14
- Contacted multiple ice cream producers across the country regarding private labeling Crumbzz ice creams

04/16/14
- Received a call back from (MN) (R) owner of (GF) Dairy Scheduled a conference call to discuss. Interested in producing Crumbzz ice cream. Don't make pints but would consider doing them for Crumbzz.

04/24/14
- Called (GF) dairy. Does private labeling and works with Whole Foods. Would love to do Crumbzz ice cream. Will do a small batch, and ship directly to Crumbzz to distribute to its clients

04/25/14
- Spoke with (MM), discussed; Packaging - does not currently do pints, but could). Would have to get machinery may take some time; Flavors - initially want two, Cinnamon Crumbler (use Crumbzz toasted crumbs and cin./streusel) and Dark Chocolate Caramel Sea Salt Quality - high end 14% butterfat; Quantity - Crumbzz opening up its product line to consumer products (originally gifts and bistro sales). He's a small producer, Crumbzz is also small (not sure of quantities-never did grocers). Will purchase pints (for retail sale) and 3 gal (for Bistro sales). (MM) will talk to his staff and get back to JSS on Tuesday 04/29/14. Did not talk about packaging.

04/29/14
- Spoke with (MM) and his team regarding Crumbzz program. Amenable to creating pints and Crumbzz flavors. Will send Crumbzz a container of their chocolate and vanilla ice creams.

05/09/14
- Received ice cream samples. JSS and team sampled both flavors; Vanilla not as sweet and tasty as ours, chocolate not as chocolaty as we would like.

05/27/14
- Sent samples of crumbs, cinnamon streusel, our ice cream and a caramel sea salt cake to (MM).
- Contacted (SW) Ice Cream Specialties (JM) re: making ice cream for Crumbzz.

5/28/14
- Received a call from (JM). Company only does large batches. Not sure if anyone in TX does small batches anymore. Decided to shelve project for the time being.

PROJECT COMPLETED

Contract with a butter producer for Crumbzz Consumer Products Division (retail sales) Cinnamon Streusel butter (for waffles)

05/22/14
- Emailed (TW) of TFPm regarding producing Crumbzz streusel and lemon butters
- Contacted (HMF) Left Message, re: creating and packaging Crumbzz Cinnamon Streusel and lemon butter.
- Acquired a list of co-packers at:XXXX. Called the following co-packing companies to get pricing and capability:
- Left Message, XXXXX Foods, (DB)
- Left Message, (TYO) Baking Company, (GC)
- 5/23/14 Spoke with (DB) of (HMF) Specialty Foods (see above) regarding streusel and lemon butters. Does private label, different types of butter for

airlines, bread companies and restaurants. Will send out samples of the type of packaging he does.

05/23/14
- (TW) reply: "We can give you some tentative pricing based on the butter and cinnamon streusel mixture. I need the recipe so I can cost this out for you. The cost if the packaging will have to be added on.
- Requested and received graphic for butter containers from (DBS)

05/27/14
- Received packaging samples from (DB) of (HFS) Specialty Foods. Received 1 oz white, 1.25 oz clear, 1.5 oz white 1.5 oz choc. and 2 oz clear. Look ideal for our use.

05/28/14
- Called LM for (DB National Accounts Mgr) to get pricing

05/30/14
- Inquired with three coffee pac sealing companies regarding the purchase of a machine to pack our own butters. Also inquired with two butter packing machine companies

06/12/14
- Received pricing on (LLC) coffee machines. Not sure if they can do butter and meet health dept requirements
- Received pricing on butter packing machines from (ADN) and (RY). Pricing for machines does not justify purchase.

PROJECT COMPLETED

Select and design Tasting Pavilion POS

06/18/11
- Review 7 systems and select POS system for tasting pavilion

09/25/11
- Spoke with (AB) of (GW) systems. discussed pricing, support, equip, capabilities (and limitations) and

availability of system
10/20/11
- Selected (GW) system
11/06/11
- Installed (GW) system
12/29/11
- Completed install and testing of (GW) POS system

PROJECT COMPLETED

BRANDING/PACKAGING

Design and order Minizz cake and shipping boxes
04/27/10
- Requested prices from XXXXXXXX Boxes (CB)
04/29/10
- Discussed styles with XXXXXXXXXX (CPS) & XXXXXXX (AP). Requested prices from CPS & AP
05/19/10
- Received sample boxes from AP
06/09/10
- Requested prices from CPS
06/10/10
- Received pricing from CB
06/23/10
- Provided logo to CPS
07/14/10
- Received updated pricing from CB
07/16/10
- Received pricing from CPS
07/27/10
- Received updated pricing from CPS
08/03/10
- Requested prices from XXXXXXXXX (SG)
08/05/10
- Received pricing from SG

8/07/10
- Requested shipping box pricing from SG. Forwarded logo to SG

08/09/10
- Requested updated cake box pricing from SG. Received updated cake box pricing from SG

08/18/10
- Requested shipping cost estimates from SG

08/20/10
- Reviewed all price estimates and awarded contract to SG. Sent PO to SG

08/23/10
- Sent TX Sales & Use Tax permit to SG

09/09/10
- Received art work for shipping boxes

089/09/10
- Approved shipping boxes

09/13/10
- Provided Sales & Use Tax Resale Cert to SG

09/23/10
- Approved updated shipping box dimensions to allow for 1-cake & 2-Minizz

09/27/10
- Notified by SG, boxes in. Picked up 12 boxes of each for testing & photo shoots.

12/02/10
- Asked SG to produce sample (and price out) of single cake and single Minizz boxes. Will have by 12/6/10

12/06/10
- Received pricing.

12/10/10
- Placed order for Cake and Minizz Trio gift boxes

02/02/11
- Received initial order of cake gift boxes

PROJECT COMPLETED

Create Gift and Perfection cards (include personal note card)

09/07/10
- Completed design for Gift and Perfection Through Commitment cards
- Chose and purchased paper for Perfection cards from XXXX (OKP) Final Cost: $XXXX (2K)
- Chose and purchased paper for Gift card from XXXX (DL)

09/08/10
- Delivered sheets to (DL)
- Completed design for interior copy of Gift Card

09/15/10
- Gift Cards printed on incorrect stock. Brought card samples to XXXX (MP) to bid out
- Perfection Cards completed by (DL)

09/20/10
- Received bid from (MP) on 8 ml thickness. (MP) to print a few samples for JSS to sign off on. Will have sample ready on 09/27/10. Upon approval need 2-days to print
- Called XXXX of (DL). Updated him on progress

09/27/10
- (MP) did not get paper from (OKP). Will have tomorrow. JSS can see sample either 09/28-09/29

09/28/10
- Picked color sample and decided on White paper. Will have ready 10/04/10

o 10/04/10
- Gift Card printing completed by (MP). JSS to pick up 10/05/10. Received final cost: $XXX 2,400 K (includes $XX one-time art fee and $XX. for paper White Vellum Bristol). NOTE: $XX per 1k at (OKP)

10/05/10
- Picked up gift cards at (MP) and dropped off at (DL) to complete gold leaf. Will be ready on 10/06/10
- Picked up completed Perfection Through

Commitment cards from (DL). Received final cost: $XXX for 2K

10/06/10
- Picked up completed Gift Cards from (DP). Received final cost: Gift Card $XXX 2,400 K (includes $XX one-time die fee)

11/08/10
- Completed "Baked By" & "Date" template for back of "Perfection Through Commitment" cards

PROJECT COMPLETED

Complete box ribbon designs and procure ribbons
04/20/10
- Called Ralph at (RL) Loved the ribbon he was using on his shirts. Asked where I could get it

04/26/10
- Ralph's personal assistant called (RL) said ribbons were purchased in India from ASI. Provided contact info

04/29/10
- Requested ribbon design and samples from (CPS)

05/05/10
- Decided on ribbon design utilizing (RL's) Jacquard ribbon for boxes o 06/09/10
- Requested prices from CPS

06/23/10
- Provided logo to CPS
- Requested prices from ASI
- Provided logo to ASI

07/07/10
- Provided ribbon requirements to ASI
  - USE - Single ribbon across center of box (cake and Minizz). Joined at top by wax seal
  - DESIGN – Black ribbed w/ tan border, logo and copy (see sample ribbon provided)
  - MATERIAL- Jacquard

- COPY – Crumbzz Logo spaced 2 inches apart
- SIZE – Ribbon width - ½" • ASI felt logo too big for ribbon

07/09/10
- Sent updated drawing of logo design. Requested update on status
- Can't do logo

07/12/10
- Decided on Crumbzz and Simply Natural
- Myriad Pro Regular for font

07/15/10
- Requested mock up

07/16/10
- Received mock up

07/20/10
- Approved w/requested change
- Increase space between each word from 2" to 3"
- ASI requested Jacquard swatch sample to match
- Sent swatch

07/21/10
- Requested DBS do mock up of ribbon ½" and 1" • Received mock ups
- Provided to ASI

07/26/10
- ASI requested Tax ID form and Trademark/Logo Release form

07/27/10
- Received updated pricing from CPS • Sent executed forms

08/02/10
- Received updated estimate

08/03/10
- Requested price correction to agree with original estimate
- Sent 50% deposit

08/05/10
- Sent resale and fed tax forms as requested

08/09/10
- Signed off on final approval

08/20/10
- Notified of shipment delay

08/23/10
- Left ASI, email requesting ETA
- ASI emailed back - 1-day delay. Airlifted on Monday, scheduled for arrival on Wednesday rest depends on US customs

08/31/10
- Picked up ribbon

PROJECT COMPLETED

Review and order shrink-wrap and shrink wrap and machine

09/17/10
- Located two suppliers of machines. Received pricing. Created price comparison chart between (FS) & (UL)
- Need to decide on heat gun or free standing machines
- Spoke with XXXXX w/(FS). Decided on 16" X 4375' 60-guage poly olefin shrink wrap film from (FS) ($XXX)

09/24/10
- Mary confirming that film is FDA approved.

09/27/10
- 14" X 500' PVC Shrink Wrap Film 75-gauge PVC Shrink Wrap Film (is both FDA food compliant and Kosher) from (FS) ($XX)
- Ordered Deluxe Super Sealer - 18" kit (incl. heat gun) from (FS) $XXXX 2-3 day shipping

09/30/10
- Received shrink wrap film

10/05/10
- Received Deluxe Super Sealer w/heat gun

PROJECT COMPLETED

Order Ancillary packaging items (Gold logo labels, tissue paper, bubble wrap and sealing tape and gold address labels)

09/30/10
- Created packaging price comparison
- Contacted four providers (NW), (SG), (UL), (PM). Pulled prices off websites. Based on pricing comparisons, selected
- (PM) for tissue paper
- (UL) for labels
- (SG) for bubble wrap and sealing tape

10/01/10
- Placed order with (PM) for tissue paper
- Placed order for labels, bubble wrap and sealing tape with (SG)

10/12/10
- Received proofs for labels from (SG)
- Requested changes

10/13/10
- Received updated proofs from (SG)

10/14/10
- Received invoice from (SG)
- Pricing dispute. Cancelled label order • Ordered labels from (UL)

10/20/10
- Received 1.5" gold labels

10/21/10
- Called (UL) regarding status on 2.5" labels. Shipped. Due in 10/21/10. Also asked status (email/RD) on sealing tape and bubble wrap. Received reply that tape and bubble wrap are in. Requested invoice for same ASAP to effect pick up

10/23/10
- Asked for invoice on tape and bubble wrap (2nd request). Requested availability answer by 10/25/10 or will purchase elsewhere

10/25/10
- Picked up sample bubble wrap & sealing tape from (SG)
- Ordered # XXXX Gold 2 5/8" X 1" Gold address labels from (UL)

10/28/10
- Received # XXXX Gold 2 5/8" X 1" Gold address labels from (UL)

10/30/10
- Created Crumbzz address label for inside of cake boxes using # XXXX Gold 2 5/8" X 1" Gold address labels from (UL)

PROJECT COMPLETED

Design and order Minizz Party Boxes (Hold 10-20 Minizz cakes. Use for party boxes and POP displays for specialty stores.

10/10/13
- Viewed different boxes to get ideas for Minizz Party Boxes

11/13/13
- Found great wine boxes at Spec's that would work great as Minizz Party Boxes. Took pictures.

12/10/13
- Found boxes at Formaggio's (client of Crumbzz). Got contact info. on box producer

12/12/13
- Contacted box producer: (DWP) Mfg. Spoke with (JW) GM. Sent email on spec's : Want display on the inside of the top of the box, would have the crumbzz logo and the words "MinizzTM Snack Crumb Cakes". The Crumbzz logo would also be on the front of the box. The inside of the top of the box would be used as the display as well. We are partial to the wood burring method similar to the attached photos. The top of the box would slide into a groove (as shown). The groove must be at an angle to compensate for the riser angle to allow for easy viewing. The dimensions of the box

would be: 9" W X 9" L X 5" D, with a 4" riser in the back. Moto Formaggio recommended you to us. As we are moving forward soon on this project, please have someone contact us ASAP.

01/10/14
- Received basic (pre-customization) pricing on 9X9X5 boxes from (DFP)

01/18/14
- Received sample boxes w/logos from (DFP).

02/03/14
- Received private branding prices $XXX per brand to create. Want one Crumbzz & another Crumbzz Logo + Minizz Snack Cakes

02/07/14
- Placed order

02/13/14
- Provided adt'l; info on box design: "Crumbzz Minizz Crumb Cakes logo to be on the lid so that when the lid is slipped into the groove it shows for display purposes. The Crumbzz (only) logo should be on the front and two sides."

02/27/14
- Received pict of finished boxes. Approved box design. OK'd order to be processed and shipped

03/02/14
- Received boxes

PROJECT COMPLETED

Develop Retail Consumer Packaging (RCP)
08/15/13
- Met with (RDV) of (SG) regarding RCP. Discussed offerings and box size requirements. Was referred to packaging graphic artist (MS) of the (H Agency).

08/30/13
- Spoke with (MS) regarding the RCP items we expect to offer. Sent (MS) product specifics.

09/03/13

- Received bid (agreement) from (MS) $XXXX. Also received email from (RDV) "Cost for mock ups to be determined once art is approved, not to exceed $XXXX."

09/05/13
- (MS) asked for logo's, images, and other deliverables as outlined in the agreement

9/17/13
- Provided nutritional labels to (MS) o 9/20/13
- Requested the following from (MS): Project description: To design packaging for frozen cakes (10" & Minizz Trio's), waffles and ice cream products; Business challenge: To develop packaging that reflects the Crumbzz upscale brand to aid in the marketing to grocers such as central market, whole foods, etc.; That can build on the Crumbzz brand (see website) and the natural ingredients they use; Item 1 Frozen 10 inch round cake packaging; Item 2 Frozen 2 inch square Minizz (three to a package) packaging; Item 3 Frozen waffle packaging; Item 4 Frozen ice cream packaging; Consumer insight: Upscale busy young professionals (millennial's – Gen X) and baby boomers; Design instructions: Review current packaging at grocers (whole foods/central market) to fit with in the current case restrictions; (A) Waffle packaging needs to accommodate 6 waffles 2 waffles to a pkg. Must also include packaging and area for cinnamon topping (0.8 ounce); (B) Minizz packaging to hold three 2 inch square cakes; (C) ice cream to be in pint size packaging ; (D) all packaging to utilize Crumbzz colors (green, beige, black, white)

10/11/13
- Received first .pdf comps on packaging

10/19/14
- Sent ice cream (Crumbler) and waffle photos to (MS)

10/22/13
- Received photos from (TH). Sent final photos (waffles)

to (MS)

11/4/13
- Reviewed mechanicals. Requested that he add Techmar name address "Manufactured by", add © Techmar, Updated waffle directions and cake & Minizz directions, add "Frozen Product. Please keep frozen" quote to ice cream and Caramel Sea Salt nutritional label

11/7/13
- Asked (MS) to add QR Code

11/7/13
- (MS) provided updated mechanicals and asked for weights of products (Missing)

12/11/13
- Received waffles mechanicals

01/12/14
- Received Mechanical files from (MS)

01/15/14
- Provided updates on mechanicals

02/10/14
- Final Mechanicals from (MS) sent to (RDV)

2/21/14
- Met with (RDV) to review box sizes. Made several changes. (RDV) to get back to JSS in 3-4 days

2/28/14
- Called (RDV) on new box sizes. Will set up meeting when completed.

03/01/14
- Met with (RDV) on new box sizes. Approved. Will have (MS) adjust mechanicals to match new sizes

03/3/14
- Asked for Mock-up photos to present to our retailers

03/05/14
- Received mock-ups from (MS)

3/16/14
- Asked to correct nutritional copy (fuzzy). (MS) asked

for original work (not pdf's)

3/18/14
- Re-built nutritional's

3/20/14
- Asked (DBS) to create .eps files on nutritional's

4/08/14
- Received final nutritional files from (DBS)

04/10/14
- Sent (MS) the final nutritional files (excluding the ice cream) for mock up creation. Asked that he review FDA site to assure correct formatting

04/11/14
- Discussed formatting of nutritional's specifically the serving sizes

04/14/14
- Received 4 of the nutritional labels for approval o

04/15/14
- JSS approved. Received all final nutritional's except waffles and ice cream. (MS) asked for ice cream ingredients

04/17/14
- Approved all to go to printer except ice cream

04/25/14
- Received pricing from (RDV) on individual boxes:
- All prices are 2 out which means you can combo 1 / 1

Funding Requirement
- 2500 @.XXX ea. 1000 Streusel 800 Caramel Sea Salt $XXX
- 2500 @.XXX ea. 500 Chocolate 200 Raspberry $XXX
- 2500 @.XXX ea. 2500 Minizz $XXX
- 2500 @.XXX ea. 2500 Waffles $XXX
- Streusel butter containers ?
- Dies $XXXX 4 = $XXX
- Total Funding Requirements $XXXXX

5/1/14
- Spoke with (RDV) . He still needs barcodes to complete the boxes.

05/28/14
- Provided licensed bar codes

06/03/14
- Received final mechanicals

PROJECT COMPLETED

Complete food photo shoot
08/29/10
- Reviewed food photos to decide on food photographer. Reviewed 16 different photographers work o 10/17/10
- Decided on (TH)

10/29/10
- Contacted (TH)

11/16/10
- Met with TH of (FF)
- Agreed to a contract on stylist and photography (Price $XXXXXX all in, $XXXX deposit, $XXXX upon acceptance of completed photos, $XXX per photo for any additional photos shot for 2011. Price includes: 9 photos; 4 cake (Streusel, Fruit, Chocolate, Pear) and 4 Minizz (Streusel, Fruit, Chocolate, All three); Also JSS PR shot (JSS on bed of Crumbzz Cakes); 1 Poster/brochure cover and POS cover shot and slice inset from cake w/fork. Terms: Crumbzz to have universal use exclusive rights to all photos, (TH) to provide price for purchase of photos (if JSS sells business).
    - Photo shoot to begin 11/18/10 and be completed 11/20/10. JSS to get DVD with photos at completion, JSS to film photo shoot 11/18/10
- Day-1 of photo shoot w/ (TH of (FF)
    - Brought 6 cakes (2 of each) and 24 Minizz (8 of each) and accoutrements. Shot 5 cake photos

for use on website. Choc landing page of site & order page (close up). Streusel landing page of site & order page (close up). Apricot landing page of site & order page (close up). Raspberry landing page of site & order page (close up). Pear landing page of site & order page (close up)

11/19/10
- Day-2 of photo shoot w/ (TH) of (FF) all three Minizz and 1 each for landing page and order page of site. Shot cake w/ slice insert for landing page, posters, tri-fold and show booth. Shot PR piece of JSS laying on top of crumbs
    - Paid photographer check for services

11/22/10
- Discussed pr photo requirements with (JL) of (MMG). Will complete for review by 11/ 26/10

11/24/10
- Received DVD with all photo's from (TH) of (FF)

PROJECT COMPLETED

Complete photo shoot for t-shirts and JSS blog

07/12/09
- Discussed t-shirt and JSS blog photo shoot w/(AC) Agreed on $XXX price

07/23/09
- Discussed food photo shoot. Agreed on price, additional $XXX

08/04/10
- Completed JSS Blog photo shoot

08/11/10
- Received proof sheet on JSS Blog photo shoot

08/12/10
- Product photo shoot w/(AC)

08/20/10
- Received proofs on Blog shoot

08/24/10

- Met with (AC) to review photography. Received final header shot for blog

08/25/10
- Received Tux shots (#152)

08/26/10
- Received the rest of JSS Blog shots (#63) 09/23/10. Awaiting t-shirts to complete t-shirt photo shoot

10/23/10
- Called (AC) to sched. Pkg. photo shoot. Sched. for 10/29/10

10/26/10
- Completed photo shoot on packaging

12/01/10
- Emailed (AC) that JSS ready to photograph t-shirts

12/05/10
- Discussed requirements 3 girls, two guys, 5 shirts & 1 photo of all eating cake. Priced $XXX per person

12/06/10
- Sent picts of T-shirts and picts on photo ideas for each shirt to (AC). Asked for acceptable shoot dates

12/19/10
- (AC) suggested week of 12/27/10.

12/26/10
- (AC) can't get models (as promised). JSS will try and locate models. AC available 01/4-5

01/10/11
- JSS found models. Christie, Diana & friend. 2 models from DBS work. Asked Diana to stage shoot. Provided photos of JSS ideas to Diana. Diana will stage

01/13/11
- Shoot set for 01/18/11

01/18/11
- Photo shoot completed. Reviewed photos w/(AC). Sent chosen photos to (AC) for touch up

01/19/11

- Received complete photo set from (AC)

PROJECT COMPLETED

Create photo for magazine cover for "THE KING OF CRUMBS" project

11/14/10
- Met with (TH) of (FF). Agreed to a contract . JSS PR shot (JSS on bed of Crumbzz Cakes). 1 Poster/brochure cover and POS cover shot. Terms: (1) Crumbzz to have lifetime universal use exclusive rights to all photos ; (2) (TH) to provide price for purchase of photos (if JSS sells business); (3) Photo shoot to begin 11/18/10 and be completed 11/20/10; (4) JSS to get DVD with photos at completion

11/19/10
- Day-2 of photo shoot w/ (TH) of (FF). Brought chef coat and suit. Shot PR piece of JSS laying on top of crumbs. Paid photographer for services

11/22/10
- Discussed pr photo requirements with (JL) of (MMG). Didn't think photo would work as designed. Suggested reclining shot (versus laying flat shot)

11/24/10
- Received DVD with photo from (TH) of (FF)

01/10/11
- Scheduled photo shoot with (AC). Will include magazine cover shot in with fashion shoot

01/13/11
- Shoot set for 01/18/11

01/18/11
- Photo shoot completed. Reviewed photo w/(AC). (AC) to remove chair for final

01/19/11
- Received completed photo from (AC)

01/20/11
- Sent photo to (JL) to insert crumb cakes

02/01/11
- Received photo (JSS on one cake) not acceptable. Created image (in Photoshop) of JSS on multiple cakes. Sent to (JL). Asked that he place shadows in appropriate placed and return as finished photo

02/13/11
- Met w/ (JL) and received finished photo. Looks good, accepted

PROJECT COMPLETED

Design and price out show booth

11/11/10
- Called (BP) of (TEP) regarding the design of a show booth. Discussed requirements. (BP) suggested we view existing materials (companies who leave their booths after contracts expire. Booth's are no longer used. Should be able to obtain substantial cost savings)

11/22/10
- Reviewed materials in stock (no longer used by previous clients). Found two towers (which will need Plexiglas top's installed), 1 center tower with Plexiglas top (requires painting bottom black), 1 8' display (will require graphic skin) and ancillary lighting
- Bryan will get price for each pc (will charge JSS cost on skins). Bryan will get back to JSS on the week of 11/29/10

12/06/10
- Pinged (BP) on pricing of booth

12/16/10
- Received prices, as follows:
  - 3x3 Curved V-Burst Frame & Case $XXX
  - V-Burst 8-color skin $XXX
  - Case-2-counter Fitted Skin $XX
  - (4)20x20x22Cubs$XXX
  - (2) 20x20x42 Cube $XXX (I called around and

this is a specialty item and you either have them custom made or rent them)
- 6' table cover $XXX
- (2) Plexy Minizz w/light $XXX (without light)
- Round Light Display case $XXX purchase, or $XXX rental; plus pull & prep labor and freight (you will need to make a 1 time purchase of a create to ship it in)
- Black Powder Coating $XXX
- Motorized display $XXX ($XXX is just for the motor)
- (2) Burst Booth Lights $XXX
- # 7 is w/out the light included in the price; when we last talked about it the prices I had for lights where too expensive so I left that price off and #9 is the powder coating @ $XXX.

PROJECT COMPLETED

Create Answering recordings for Crumbzz corporate and bistro
03/28/14
- Reviewed online recording services. Found Fiverr site Reviewed voices found one that will work. Selected voice
  Contacted talent, awaiting a reply.

04/25/14
- Contracted with (R13). Wrote script. sent to (R13) to record.

PROJECT COMPLETED

MARKETING/PUBLIC RELATIONS/SALES

Get website up and running
08/17/10
- Reviewed different website developers for Crumbzz

website Shopping cart must be able to handle multiple orders with multiple gift cards, shipped to multiple addresses and allow for integration with UPS, FedEx and USPS. Also allow for discounting and wholesale order placement. Settled on (H) to develop site.

08/23/10
- Agreed to terms on price and time frame to completion of website with (H). Paid 1/3 down to commence build.

o 09/08/10
- Provided (H) with actual inventory of all items for sale. Asked to include blog address link on site

09/14/10
- Reminded (H) to allow input of discount codes

09/21/10
- (H) stated "have the basic ordering system working...will upload the basic ordering system for your review this evening... For the bulk and wholesale orders, I will need more time"

09/22/10
- (H) stated "I have uploaded the forms and am now running the scripts to set up your database and populate it with data. Once this has finished I will update you again and send documentation"

09/27/10
- (H) stated, "The dev site is up with the basic shopping cart. I am adding the connection to an Authorize.Net test account so you can create test orders and will update you when it's ready"

09/30/10
- Received admin credentials to access website and update copy and photos. Admin login credentials included username: XXXXXXX and password XXXXXXX. Requested Login ID and password to Authorize.Net account. Provided Login ID and password to Authorize.Net account

10/04/10
- Updated copy on all pages except ordering and t-shirt pages. Asked (H) to provide access to these pages to update

10/06/10
- Received instructions on photo upload procedure. Uploaded latest changes, testing

10/07/10
- Asked for update (H)

10/08/10
- Gave (CB) (webmaster) the website project. Will keep (H) working on what he is doing as well as (CB) doing website as well. Will have completed before 11/15/10
- Asked for ETA from (H)
- (CB) requested typical Excel spread sheet client would provide for bulk orders. JSS provided as requested.

10/10/10
- Received ETA of 10/11/10 from (H) o 10/11/10
- No "completed site" notification from (H) o 10/14/10
- Explained tea/coffee ordering process to (CB) o

10/17/10
- Discussed adding html5 element to home page (approved). Adding sub menu for heart & soul pages.

10/21/10
- Asked (CB) for update on site progress. "Site seems to be coming along well… just trying to get every thing on there at the moment then I can play around with it" I was thinking of maybe using the home page to announce winners and specials… what do you think? "Not a prob. I'm with you on simple easy user interface that gets to the point. Just want to make sure all is done tastefully."

11/02/10
- Asked (CB) for update on site progress

11/04/10
- Asked (CB) for update on site progress. On schedule, needs SSL and FTP info to move forward. Committed

to providing by c.o.b. 11/04/10.
- JSS called Go Daddy to get required info. Required to activate SSL (won't have number for 72 hrs). Consolidated SSL, crumbzz.com domain and hosting service expirations to 2013. Forwarded crumbzz.net to crumbzz.com. Created ftp login user name (CB) and password (XXXXXX) for (CB) to access acct
- Provided info for FTP and Password to JSS Go Daddy account to (CB). Asked (CB) to change Oct launch to Nov launch date on temp landing page. Received email from (CB) "Thanks for the FTP info... I am a little confused on one part. I was able to log on and get to the ftp site...however, once I logged on (and I tried with two different programs and multiple different attacks) I could see no files on the server... this is odd because there should at least be one... the coming soon page. I'm not sure if it's a case of the account you set up for me not having access to that file, or what... but I am unable to change that page with out being able to access that file. (CB) has complete"root" access, shouldn't be happening

10/05/10
- Called Go Daddy to see how this is possible. Told to Assign (CB) as an Acct Exec. Assigned Acct Exec. Good to go. Temp holding page updated to show Nov

11/7/10
- (CB) having some issues with items for sale. Discussed specidics on all, plus site readiness by 11/15/10. Will be ready except for back-end functionality (which will be ready a few days after). Told (CB) will have several changes, he will do until back-end up and running. Asked (CB) not to forget online ordering page for corporate gifting. Provided hand out page that we are currently using. No need to tie into merchant account, just email JSS whenever an order is placed. Will create ASAP

11/09/10

- Reviewed temporary online ordering form.
- Got rates from Fed Ex. Asked (CB) to insert. Once inserted, form good to go
- Reviewed progress of website. Decided to change intro page to much more stylish/graphic a page. Ordering page up and running!

11/13/10
- Received email from (CB). Running behind schedule

11/14/10
- Informed (CB) that 8.25% sales tax in state of TX was missing. Sales tax request completed

11/21/10
- Received update on website progress and request for additional info for website final build out: Received the following: Crumbzz - ToDo : Need from JSS: - 72 assorted items!

11/22/10
- Provided all requested information to (CB)

11/23/10
- Discussed status of photos with (TH). Will have completed by 4 pm Friday. Asked what size and type (horizontal/vertical) we needed. JSS will check w/ (CB).
- Discussed status of site w/ (CB). Confident he will be done soon. Discussed photo session and landing page design. Asked about size and type. (CB) would like to see photos before he completes design. Asked (CB) to send his design ideas for the landing page and ordering pages. Will send those as well as URL for site tonight.
- Called (TH) (photographer) asked him to send to JSS and (CB) photos so (CB) could see what to design to (TH) will provide morning of 11/24/10

11/24/10
- Received photos from (TH)
- Provided photos for ordering page and landing page of website to (CB). Provided 2 slides on idea for

landing page to (CB). Ideas show landing page and close up of product description
- Asked (JL) of (MMG) if he could split out photos (no backgrounds). Not a problem

11/27/10
- Told (CB), (JL) would be prepping photos for site. Asked if he needed anything special done for the ordering photos. Also asked how he intended to set up ordering page and what was the status of site.

11/28/10
- Met w/ (JL). Provided photos (master file) to have (JL) strip out photos. Will have bid to complete job by 12 noon 11/29/10
- Updated (CB) on status

11/29/10
- Received bid from (JL) $XX for JSS shot, $XXX for all other shots. Approved. Will have by 12/3/10

11/30/10
- Sent order form issue (missing info) to (CB). Reviewed, can't replicate issue. Asked (CB) to add "Same as billing" box above shipping address. Asked (CB) to update temp landing page replace Nov with Dec. Reviewed new home landing page idea (fade in) approved

12/2/10
- Asked (CB) to provide a link (box) on the temporary landing page to the www.jstephensadler.com blog. Should say "Crumbzz behind the scene's look"
- Spoke with (JL). Photos will begin coming over to (CB) today. Provided (CB)'s contact info so John can discus required format

12/04/10
- (CB) asked how to lay out shadows. Asked (JL) to assist (JL) can discuss required format

12/27/10
- Provided (CB) with FED EX registration info to assimilate

Fed Ex into the site. (JL) can discuss required format

01/03/11
- Got email from (CB) site ready for review. Requested check in amount of $XXXX. (2/3) pmt due. (JL) can discuss required format

01/04/11
- Reviewed site w/ (CB). Sent check. Will get back to (CB) with requests for changes. (JL) can discuss required format

01/15/11
- Reviewed site on iPad at Apple store. Looks good

01/17/11
- Sent first of several emails regarding change requests

01/21/11
- Asked (CB) for his web development website address (for assimilation on my blog)
- Sent (HW) (wax seal) assimilation requirements for Crumbzz website (included flow process)

01/22/11
- Sent final review change request (8 email set)

01/24/11
- Asked for status update
- "Other then the ordering process, voting and recipe entry sections (which I can't get into) these are my final notes on my initial review of the site. Asked to change the temp landing page from Dec to Feb"
- Received reply from (CB): The issues that you've been having logging in and stuff on the site is because I was working on backend stuff. I've been trying to not upload a whole bunch of new stuff because I knew you have been going through everything. I'll let you know when I put more up"

01/30/11
- Replied to (CB)'s email:
- I am doing my best to assure our going live before Friday... I am just frustrated with myself right now.

02/05/11
- Sent (CB) ASP.net change notice

02/06/11
- (CB) stated that he made excellent progress on site
- Reviewed site, noted a lot of updates have been made

02/07/11
- Sent (CB) my review notes to update site

02/08/11
- Reviewed entire site w/(CB) (page by page)
- Made on-the-fly changes. JSS to send notes on rest. Discussed Excel spread sheet requirements. Discussed wholesale ordering section. Reviewed voting process requirements. Asked to make sure blog link on all pages of site. Sent gift card example (need two fill in spots). 1 Sent Club Page body and header copy. Sent wax seal copy and header. Agreed to move wax seals to reserve your now section. Provided updated pricing. Provided checkout pict

02/09/11
- Provided return and privacy policy copy for new section
- Provided Restaurant caution message:
- The following message needs to be placed by all restaurant prices in the wholesale section "IT IS A VIOLATION OF CRUMBZZ POLICY AND FDA LABELING REQUIREMENTS TO OFFER RESTAURANT PACKAGED PRODUCTS FOR OFF PREMISES CONSUMPTION. VIOLATION MAY RESULT IN FDA FINES, OPERATING LICENSE FORFEITURE AND TERMINATION OF PRODUCT AVAILABILITY."

02/10/11
- Received invoice for final payment

02/11/11
- Sent final payment ($XXX)

02/14/11
- Received update from (CB): "made some big

improvements that I think you're really gonna like. I've had to totally redo the database in order to make it work though... I also upgraded the library that we're using and made it so it's now gonna be easier to update in the future... I'm not able to put them on the server yet because when I did all this I didn't spend time updating the coming soon section and these changes will break that completely. I still have a handful of notes to complete and I'm spending most of today trying to get those done. My biggest hurdle was getting the database reconfigured, which (I hope) was finally completed yesterday. Today is about incorporating the new information we have available to include the features we discussed."
- Crumbzz video completed. Sent video type request from (MN) to (CB). (CB) reply: "I would like it in two formats if possible. MP4 + H.264, with ACC or MP3. MP4 is the highest priority of the two though. YouTube size (640x480) is fine."

02/16/11
- Asked for update on site status. Waiting on photos from (JL)
- Updated (CB) to that fact, pinged (JL) on ETA of photos
- Received reply from (JL) on ETA "These are the files left to send. I will send them by noon tomorrow. 1. Add shadows: Spatula 170 john (girl kneeling). 2. Remove background and add shadows: Page 3C 2[1]

02/17/11
- Received final photos from (JL). Provided all to (CB) via cloud server and email

02/18/11
- Received final bill from (JL). Reviewed final updates (change a couple of pictures and add password protected confirmation by specialty store for each c client order. Hopes to be done by 02/20/11

02/22/11

- Got email from (D) (Wax Seal company) "I just checked with (M) and he hasn't heard back from (CB). Please give me a quick update when you have a moment." Forwarded (D)'s email to (CB) asking him to follow up

02/23/11
- Asked status of site. Received following answer "I'm gonna call (D) tomorrow about the wax seals. Once that's figured out all I have before we go live (unless I'm mistaken) is just formatting the email that gets sent to you after ever order. The things that we won't have at first is the Specialty Order Page.
- Received email from (D) "We got a call today from (CB). I think he has all the info. I have asked him to contact me directly if he needs more details or clarification.

02/27/11
- Website up and running (except for specialty ordering and voting). Issues with FedEx shipping and Authorize.net, credit card charging integration. Also have problems with nav bar on some versions of Internet explorer. Provided (CB) with two clients screen shots to understand issue

03/01/11
- Credit card integration issues corrected. Shipping and nav bar issues still remain. Provided (CB) with one of the client's who have nav bar issues to work with (LJ) of XXXX Payments System

03/02/11
- Received an email to (CB), from (LJ) from her tech dept. (SL # BALTIMORE) "The shopping cart is not secured. They are taking payment over an unencrypted page."

03/03/11
- Discussed ie7 issues. Because site built in html5, won't run properly on ie 7 or older. Since ie 9 is sched. to be released shortly, decided to provide a pop-up

that states that the site runs best on ie 8 + to upload ie for FREE select link. Will link to MS ie download.
- Other than ie issue, secure payment has been corrected as well as the shipping issues. Site is now good to go except for the following: Back-end Specialty/Restaurant ordering (including Excel spreadsheet upload). Voting. Video link. (CB) to work on outstanding issues in the order stated above

03/09/11
- Asked (CB) for the status of site

03/15/11
- Handed off (LO) (FSC) (see pr) to (CB). • Asked status of site. No reply.

05/07/11
- Asked status of site. No reply.

05/25/11
- Since developer has walked off without completing site, contracted with 1 Shopping cart to handle sites shopping cart. Because our back-end access is so restricted, have contracted with (DL), another developer, to handle updates as needed.

PROJECT COMPLETED

Get Facebook, and Twitter sites up
09/12/10
- Called (RG) (recommended by SVM). Set up meeting (09/24/10) to work on Twitter/Facebook sites. (RG) cancelled the 09/24 meeting. No further action

09/20/10
- Met with (CL) re: Facebook and Twitter launches. Will come back with a proposal. Never got back with a proposal. No further action

09/21/10
- Spoke with (CB) regarding Facebook and Twitter launches. Scheduled to review and call JSS back on 09/23/10

09/24/10

- Called asked why app's not up. Will start immediately w/Facebook and Twitter pages. Want pages separate from JSS personal pages. JSS provided user names, passwords to access Facebook and Twitter accounts to (CB)

10/01/10
- Twitter and Facebook accounts up and running

10/19/10
- Met with (DM) the Technical Director & Developer of (CS) (at Meetup meeting) on proposed pr and social network plan. Apologized for lack of contact. Will get ball moving. Received a weekly meeting maker request, accepted

10/23/10
- Received (CS).com proposal

10/26/10
- Sent proposal back to (CS) requesting a few minor changes to the proposal. Asked to include not only the process, but also the expected results. Received new conference number XXXXXXXX. Met on proposal. Requested milestones and value statement for work. Stated that can't begin until website goes live. Also requested assistance on marketing the corporate gifting program (potential client list's). JSS to provide an email Sent email on program statement.

11/30/10
- Received specifics on the value statement (still vague.) Decided to meet when website is up to move project along
- JSS created Facebook and Twitter pages in-house

PROJECT COMPLETED

Create POS poster and hand out piece for Specialty Retailers

10/14/10
- Began work on pieces

10/15/10
- Completed POS poster, hand out, and pricing sheet. Await packaging photos

10/29/10
- Inserted photos/completed both pieces

PROJECT COMPLETED

Create order form and hand out piece for Retail Clients

11/04/10
- Completed design work on pieces. Sent pieces to first two retail clients

11/09/10
- Updated order sheet
- Provided work sheet to (CB) to create temporary online order form

PROJECT COMPLETED

Create email marketing piece (to corporations) for Corporate Gifting Program

10/26/10
- Completed hand out and pricing sheet
- Await packaging photos

10/29/10
- Inserted photos/completed piece

11/08/10
- Updated ordering form

PROJECT COMPLETED

Create Restaurant hand out piece

10/14/10
- Began work on piece

10/15/10
- Completed hand out piece and Restaurant pricing sheet
- Await packaging photos

10/29/10
> • Inserted photos/completed piece

PROJECT COMPLETED

Create marketing piece for re-sellers
10/26/10
> • Began work on piece

10/27/10
> • Completed hand out piece and Resellers pricing sheet
> • Await packaging photos

10/29/10
> • Inserted photos/completed piece

PROJECT COMPLETED

Create a Crumbzz video for Crumbzz website and You Tube use
11/14/10
> • Spoke with (MN) President of (KIMS) at (GW) meeting regarding a discounted video shoot. May do something for the entire (GW) association

11/16/10
> • (MN) announced a special $XXX offer for (GW) members (if enough members take the deal at a single days shoot at (MN) location. Told (MN) we were in

11/17/10
> • Set video shoot date for 10 AM, 12/01/10. Shoot to be at: Hope Cottage 4209 McKinney Avenue, Dallas, TX 75205-4509

11/25/10
> • Received video shoot prep document

11/30/10
> • Sent Crumbzz Product-Corp Overview for (MN) review to familiarize with the Crumbzz company. Discussed key points to be discussed in video

12/01/10
> • Filmed video. Provided (MN) with access to cloud server

to obtain Crumbzz photos for use in video o 12/02/10
- Asked (MN) when we can expect finished product
- Alerted (CB) that a video had been filmed, asked likely place on website. Home page. WJSS to advise (CB) when video is scheduled to be completed when information arrives from (MN). Received email from (MN) "Mid week next, let me know if there's a specific size/format. I can render in just about anything"
- Asked (CB) for desired format. Reply from (CB); MPEG 4

12/28/10
- Called asked status of video. Received msg behind but working on it

01/14/11
- Left vm and email… Where is video??? Received email back from (MN) "Lost a storage drive last week right before finishing and had to start over.

01/24/11
- Sent email asking where video is? Received reply back from (MN) "Finishing today, yours has been very difficult to get to the core message and edit down to a reasonable length. Sorry for the delay, but I want it to be the absolute best result for you. Thanks for your patience, M

01/25/11
- Received video for approval at: XXXXXXX

01/26/11
- Sent (MN) email with comments:
- "Viewed the video last night. Looks great except for a few tweaks. Asked to make 8 adjustments. My website will be up in 1-2 weeks and the video will be featured on it. On my blog I would like to place a link to your company. Please provide the proper link and name (label for link) you would like me to use. If you have any questions, please feel free to call me at XXX-XXX-XXXX. (MN) replied that he would make all changes. Needs a PNG or JPG of Crumbzz logo.

>   Provide JPG of logo

01/30/11
>   - Requested update on video progress. (MN) committed to a 2/2/11 ETA

02/07/11
>   - Requested video

02/0-8/11
>   - (MN) requested resend of logo as transparency

02/09/11
>   - Sent logo as PNG transparency

02/10/11
>   - Received video for review at: XXXXXXXX

02/11/11
>   - Asked (MN) to make a final change on .com (too close) and the meeting in the airport (too obscure). Provided (MN) with alternative copy to add at bottom or allowed him to add JSS audio explaining chance meeting. (MN) will add copy at bottom of segment to better explain chance encounter and add additional spacing for the .com

02/14/11
>   - Alerted (CB) (webmaster) to arrival of video. Asked (CB) what format he wanted (copied MN). (CB) replied: "I would like it in two formats if possible. MP4 + H.264, with ACC or MP3. MP4 is the highest priority of the two though." Render in 640x480

02/17/11
>   - Asked (MN) for update on status of video. Received reply from (MN): "Having major issues, possibly a corrupted file from the first version which is the baseline for the changes made. I have all the changes made and can view in my timeline but it keeps crashing my system." JSS reply: "We started this process on 11/16/10 with your offer on GW. We filmed the video on 12/01/10. That's four month's and counting. Need to have this project completed!

02/17/11

- Received reply from (MN): "Lost part of the project. I will begin rebuilding the remainder of the project tomorrow and hopefully finish sometime over the weekend." I would ask that you continue to be patient for a few more days while I complete the video. You will have received a finished product. .

02/22/11
- Asked status on video

03/02/11
- Asked status on video

05/09/11
- Filed complaint with BBB on all three of (MN)'s companies.

PROJECT COMPLETED

Start the process to get PR program going
07/01/10
- Met with (NT) at Fancy Food Show in NYC. Discussed Crumbzz. Provided Crumbzz Corp Overview

07/07/10
- Received (NT) proposal. Too much ($XXXX per mo)

09/17/10
- Purchased media lists from(MC, LLC) Dealt with (HS)

10/12/10
- Received email from (NT) of (T & Co.). Proposed an incubator program where we pay as we generate revenues 10/15/10
- Replied to (NT) that I liked the idea and would like to discuss further.

10/18/10
- Received reply that (NT) can help with all we need. Requested meeting on 10/19-10/20/10. Never received reply from (NT), sent follow up email. Never received a reply.

10/27/10
- Received email scheduled phone call for 10/29/10

10/29/10

- Never received call

11/14/10
- Sent Press Release to (KM) of The Advocate Magazine.
  Will insert in Jan issue

12/05/10
- Emailed (EH) of DFW Close Up Channel 33 KDAF-TV, a weekly TV talk show (7am Sunday's) on DFW businesses, to suggest a show on Crumbzz

01/20/11
- Scheduled 02/24/11 to film show. (EH) suggested the following: "We can talk about your crumb cakes (and taste them ☺, talk about how you are a local producer, your green efforts, and your non-profit. We have tons to talk about!"

02/24/11
- Filmed DFW Close Up TV Show for 02/27/11 show. Brought two cakes for crew. Asked for link and copy of video

02/27/11
- Received email from (EH) (host) "Hey J Stephen! What a pleasure it was to meet you and have you on DFW Closeup! I've been raving about your cakes to everyone I see! Thanks so much for helping coordinate this segment! I had a blast! Here is the embed code: XXXX. Here is the Link: XXXX

02/28/11
- JSS & DBS met with (LO) President and (FSC) regarding handling the pr for Crumbzz. (LO) will get back to JSS with a proposal this week. Left cake

03/01/11
- Received email from (LO) "Great meeting, thank you. HOLY SHIT. They were like vultures on the cake after you left........I took the remaining carcass and put it in my car so I could pass to some of my neighbors. I am going to do the blah blah blah proposal and send to you.

Obviously, there are many things that it may or may not contain, but we will figure that out as we go. It contains the basic dogma that we try and follow, but aren't necessarily committed to get the job done. I am going to set a price that I feel is fair. That said, we can discuss, and it is always open, but I think out of the gate we can get some quick momentum on this from a p.r. and general product buzz, so it is a good value for the payback with very little initial investment.
- As I said, we are pushing long lead pubs deadlines, so I will get this to you and hopefully we can come to an agreement and go from there. Also, I have done outreach to Deep Ellum guy and other property brokers to see what they have. Over and out!"

03/02/11
- Met with (EL) of (G social CRM) company. Reviewed their unified API platform services via webcast regarding:
- Linking all social services sign on with our sign in system. Single click "sharing" of posts to multiple networks; Group sharing; Community feeds for what a particular person has done e.g. who voted for what, who ordered what, etc.; Analytics, what individual users are doing, influencer rankings; One-time set up fee $XXXX; Ongoing fee's $XXXX per mo; Will contact JSS in 3rd qtr

03/04/11
- Sent email to (AR), radio host of Mother Earth News Radio (AR)- At a recent GW meeting, I spoke to (NT), the Publisher of Edible DFW Magazine. (NT) suggested that our company and specifically a project we are currently working on, would be an ideal topic for their show.

03/07/11
- Received rough draft of agreement from (LO). $XXXX for 6-month's.

03/09/11

- Asked for references. Also asked for week to week roadmap

03/10/11
- Received two references, discussed roadmap. Called both references; (DS) (Chocolatier) and (S&C) (Furniture Company). (DS) started 1-yr ago, very similar to Crumbzz. Liked what I heard.
- Contacted (LO) told her it's a go. (LO) will contact JSS 03/11/11 or 03/14/11 to get the ball rolling
- Sent introduction email to the editors of the following food & beverage magazines: (1) Art of Eating Magazine; (2) Bon Appetit Magazine; (3) Culinary Trends Magazine; (4) Fancy Food & Culinary Products Magazine; (5) Gourmet Retailer Magazine; (6) Modern Baking Magazine
- The following affluent lifestyle magazines: (1) Affluent Page Magazine; (2) Modern Luxury Dallas Magazine; (3) Panache Magazine; (4) Robb Report Magazine; (5) Selecta Magazine; (6) Signature Magazine; (7) Simply The Best Magazine; (8) Social Affairs Magazine; (9) Town & Country Magazine; (10) Upscale Magazine; (11) WSJ Magazine. Received request to participate from Modern Luxury Dallas Magazine

03/11/11
- Sent cake to Modern Luxury Dallas Magazine

03/14/11
- Initial meeting with(LO) President of (FSC) & (AC) Social Media/PR Specialist . Discussed branding, website copy, social media, potential clients, brochure design, etc.
- (LO) to get plan and copy input back to JSS ASAP
- JSS to provide (AC) with admin rights to Facebook and Twitter sites. (AC) will maintain from this point forward. Provided (AC) admin rights to all social media sites

PROJECT COMPLETED

Publicize Real Estate Corporate Gifting Program
01/05/11
- Received email from (S) @ Maudee's Café & Tea Room and (VS) of Ellen Terry would like to meet regarding offering our cakes as gifts

01/06/11
- Spoke to (VS). Set up meeting for 01/07/11

01/07/11
- Met with (VS). Set up presentation to her associates for 2/7/11 from 8-10 am to introduce Crumbzz client gifts. JSS to bring samples to taste and show packaging. Speak 15 minutes on Crumbzz & offerings. (VS) also suggested that JSS bring Ebby Halliday, (BB) (Dave Perry-Smith Realtors) and (CP) (Craig Penfold Properties/Chicago Title Insurance Co.) a cake to taste

01/15/11
- Dropped off cake to Ebby Halliday (put from (VS) to Ebby for her birthday). Spoke with Ebby and her assistant (BT) about company and offerings

01/24/11
- Received email from (JS) regarding the hiring of a new associate. Email came to JSS @ Crumbzz. Replied to email with Crumbzz Real Estate Corporate Gifting Pgm offer. Sent corporate gifting handout
- Called Ebby Halliday spoke to (BT) (Ebby's assistant). Will set up a time later in the week to discuss offering it to their clients

02/08/11
- Dropped off cakes at (BB) (Dave Perry-Smith Realtors) and (CP) (Craig Penfold Properties/Chicago Title Insurance Co.)

02/11/11
- Called eft message for (BB) (Dave Perry-Smith Realtors) and (CP) (Craig Penfold Properties/Chicago Title Insurance Co.)

02/15/11

- Spoke with (BH) regarding presenting to the Real Estate board of FL. (BH) will research and provide contact info

02/16/11
- Received contact info from (BH)

03/03/11
- Asked (VS) to alert Ellen Terry Associates that website is now up and accepting orders

PROJECT COMPLETED

Get agents for TV show based on Going Green From The Ground Up storyline
08/23/10
- Called spoke w/ (SAS). Will send approved format tonight and speak to his contacts ASAP

08/25/10
- Contact (SAS) used, Contact did nothing with story

10/15/10
- Emailed(NT) of (T) & Company Inc. with regards to possible agent contacts. Told her: I have developed a show idea on taking an old building and building from scratch a green, energy efficient bake house for Crumbzz. Love to discuss with you. Perhaps you can help me get this to the right people to help move it along. I believe this to be another excellent vehicle to get in front of the media

10/18/10
- Received reply that (NT) can help get show on air. Requested meeting on 10/19-10/20/10. Never received reply from (NT), sent follow up email. Never received a reply.

03/15/11
- Discussed Going Green from the ground up idea with (LO).
- Asked to have her get JSS on OWN (Ophra Winfrey Network). Know that they are looking for new show material.

PROJECT COMPLETED

Create Hotel hand out piece
11/05/10
- Began work on piece. Completed handout piece

PROJECT COMPLETED

Create Answering recordings for Crumbzz corporate and bistro
03/28/14
- Reviewed online recording services. Found Fiverr site Reviewed voices found one that will work. Selected voice Contacted talent, awaiting a reply.

04/25/14
- Contracted with (R13). Wrote script. sent to (R13) to record.

PROJECT COMPLETED

Get bid requests for the creation of Crumbzz Crowd funding video
04/16/14
- Sent e-mail to (PG) regarding bid request for Crumbzz project for bid on crowd funding video production

04/25/14
- Called (JC) regarding bid request for PEA and Crumbzz projects for bid on crowd funding video production

05/09/14
- Asked and received links to (PH) of (FLP)

05/10/14
- Sent (PH) the PEA brochure

05/12/14
- Conference call with (PH) provided her ideas and budget to film crowd funding commercials. Received an email regarding the bid: discussing options in terms of cost for the production, depending on the location choice,

05/13/14
- Spoke to (JDMC) (Videographer) re: production of crowd funding video (JD does DR's training video's). Sent samples of type/ look we wanted.
- Set up meeting for 05/14/14 Met with (JDMC) (Videographer) to discuss possible crowd funding video (Does DR training video's). Will provide a bid price on video's
- JSS had 1-hour meeting with (JDMC). Went over what the programs were and what we wanted. Will get back to us ASAP.

05/14/14
- Sent (JDMC) email: (JDMC).

05/15/14
- Received contract from (PH): When do you all anticipate to be our film date? Currently May 3 is available and most likely the studios I'm connected with also have availability for that day.

05/20/14
- Received the following email from (JDMC): Unable to complete by required date.

05/25/14
- Sent WPC article on crowd funding which raises concerns about our program. Agreed to hold off on video's until JSS speaks with attorney. JSS to call (PH) - of (FLP) to alert her to the change.

05/27/14
- JSS contacted (PH), informed (PH) that attorney's opinion presented some issue that will necessitate cancelling project.

PROJECT COMPLETED

ACCOUNTING/OPERATIONS/STAFFING

Complete product cost analysis
09/10/10

- Started cost analysis

10/06/10
- Completed cost analysis

PROJECT COMPLETED

Complete Inventory tracking system
09/15/10
- Started ITS

10/07/10
- Completed ITS

12/15/10
- Input all data into ITS

PROJECT COMPLETED

Create a Standard Operating Procedures (SOP) Manual
09/05/10
- Reviewed Upper Crust SOP as possible template

09/16/10
- Started crafting Crumbzz SOP

11/15/10
- Completed Crumbzz SOP

PROJECT COMPLETED

Complete Tasting Pavillion site budget and site plan
08/20/10
- Met (CT) to review space requirements. JSS to produce requirements document (space planner) for the Exposition location (include equip, layout and city requirements). Document should highlight questions to ask the City of Dallas regarding approval to use space as a bakery and flow of business and equipment requirements for (CT) to use to design space
- Met w/(DW) Property Mgr to view properties

08/21/10
- Met w/ (EC) to view space in Dallas and to discuss possible purchase of used bakery equipment

- Met w/ (LJ) Landlord to view XXX Exposition Ave space
- Met with (RC), Landlord, to view XXX Swiss Ave space

o 08/23/10
- Viewed several spaces in Deep Ellum

09/13/10
- Viewed both sites w/landlords
- Completed document and sent to (CT)

09/24/10
- Asked (CT) for drawings and inclusion of HVAC in plan costs. Will have by end of week

10/04/10
- Reviewed both sites with (CT) & HVAC vendor

10/05/10
- Reviewed both sites with (CT) & (GC). (CT) will have initial layout proposal by 10/13/10
- Met (CT) to review space requirements. JSS to produce requirements document (space planner) for the Exposition location (include equip, layout and city requirements). Document should highlight

10/06/10
- Pulled teams off Swiss Ave site. Only working with Exposition site
- Approved (CT) rough on site plan. Initial layout proposal due by 10/13/10

10/07/10
- Received basic (no build out) floor plan from (CT) Spoke with (CB) of DFW (DW). Will attefd meeting on 10/12/10 to speak to green contractors and GC's
- Received request for BTU's on equip from (CT) Input typical equipment to be used into Tasting Pavilion Equip Req file. Sent to (CT)

10/09/10
- Received drawing from (CT). Required equip will not fit in space

10/11/10

- Decided to look at location in Deep Ellum. Alerted (CT) of change. Scheduled walk-thru on 10/12/10

10/13/10
- Attended DFW (GW) Meetup made contacts w/ (MK) of (GW) contractor. Also met with (GYC) (commercial cleaning supplier) and Edible Dallas Fort Worth (food magazine publisher)

10/14/10
- Scheduled meeting (10/19/10) at Main St location to review space for a totally green build out

10/19/10
- Reviewed site w/(MK)of (EG)
- JSS to get (MK) rudimentary drawing of building with locations of department. (MK) to send JSS contact info on CA design co's that can help with design
- Asked (CT) for status of space drawing. 2-weeks out

10/20/10
- Sent drawing to (MK) Asked for CA contact numbers

10/21/10
- Told landlord at Exposition address, won't be taking space

10/22/10
- Requested CA contact #'s again from (MK)

10/31/10
- Received site plan from (CT)

11/02/10
- Received revised site plan with measurements from (CT)
- Received request from (MK) of (EG). "Working on it over the next week. Looking over the floor plan,.Asked what kind of finish out quality and style JSS looking for to determine the rough budget." Sent site plan and photos of ideas for site to (MK)

11/03/10
- Sent adt'l. picts to (MK) & (CT)

11/19/10
- Received preliminary numbers on build-out of main

street address of: $XXXX-$XXXX for the build-out, including mechanical systems & roof, not including kitchen equipment. Asked for breakdown of estimate

12/22/10
- Received cost estimate, broken down by category

12/23/10
- Decided to put project on hold until after holidays.

01/10/11
- Decided to view properties outside of the Dallas city limits

08/16/10
- Met w/ (SVM). She graciously agreed to let us use XXXX Culinary Art Center temporarily until we found a spot.

08/26/10
- Called on empty restaurant on corner of Ross & Greenville.

11/28/10
- Scheduled a meeting for 12/03/10 with Donut shop on Corner of XXXX and XXXXX to discuss the use of their facility as Crumbzz kitchen. Must have storage area.
- Received call from (MA) owner of property on Lower Greenville. Set up 3 pm meeting to view property
- Viewed property. Has walk-in refrigerator and freezer and range hood w/ grease trap, needs oven and sink and work counters. Will see if they have a sink and counter

12/02/10
- Spoke to (MA), wants $XXXXX! Not happening

01/04.11
- Called (SVM) to finalize agreement LM office phone

01/09/11
- Called (SVM) again LM cell

01/10-01/14/11
- Viewed several potential sites
- Sites must have grease trap and vent hoods to be viable

01/21/11
- Contacted SVM to alert her that we would be starting operations soon. Asked to schedule time to assimilate into center. (SVM) assistant (MC) worked out specifics. All set to go.. SVM also has a friend who bakes pastries in Oak Cliff that might be able to work something out.
  - Contacted President/CEO, Seagoville Economic Development Corporation, regarding space availability (without same restrictions as Dallas – sprinkler systems, grease pits, vent hoods, etc.) and funding programs to place our company in Seagoville. Stated that Seagoville has several grant programs and much less restrictions than Dallas. Scheduled a walk-thru on sites and discussion of programs for 01/27/11

01/26/11
- JSS previewed downtown Seagoville with (BR) Director of Economic Development. Bad shape, all buildings empty. Noted a few potential sites.

01/26/11
- Went to Oak Cliff area to view potential locations

01/27/11
- Met with (BR), previewed downtown area. Town has grant money that will pay for complete build out (including kitchen). Would love to have a company like Crumbzz help revitalize the downtown area. Spoke with
  owner of one building. Wants to sell not rent $XXXXX

01/28/11
- Received contact info from (BR) on another site

01/29/11
- Took photos of downtown

02/04/11
- Called left message for owners

02/10/11
- Info out of date. No longer at location. Called left message for (BR)

02/11/11
- Called left message for (BR)

02/14/11
- LM. Alerted (BR) to outdated info

02/15/11
- Received email from (BR) "I am back from the trade show in Anaheim and will get with you asap. Trying to catch up on a lot of things at once."

02/16/11
- Sent (BR) an email "Need to move project forward now."

02/17/11
- Set up 2 pm 02/18/11 meeting @ (BR)'s office to review. Asked that she have all owner contact info available

02/18/11
- Reviewed several more buildings in Seagoville. Came to an agreement w/ building owner on rental fee ($XXX per mo.)
- Will get call from owner to view building on Monday 02/21/11 o 02/21/11
- Emailed (BR)… no one contacted JSS. (BR) reply… will get someone on it ASAP.

02/22/11
- Received call from (JP) (Realtor) can show at 2 pm. Went to site, owners rep's came with wrong keys. Will get new keys made today. Joe will call JSS when he gets keys. Called (BR) updated her on status, asked for names of owners at corner building and building between 112 Elm and corner 111 Elm?. Will locate. Told her (JP) has name of owners of 111 Elm. (BR) will research
- Stopped at Ambassador Park Hotel 1312 S. Ervay Street (3rd time visiting hotel, never any answer at door) to see about renting kitchen. Went in basement door. Met with caretaker (BH). Set up meeting 10 am 02/23/11

02/23/11
- Met with (BH) and his wife. Toured the hotel. Reviewed storage requirements, kitchen requirements, etc. Also discussed possibility of JSS staff cooking for College dorm (which may be taking the top 3 floors of the hotel.) (BH) is meeting with CW College Friday and will call JSS by Tuesday when he knows what is required.

02/24/11
- Dropped off free cake for (BH) and his family. Received email request "the college (has) a need for 2 meals per day. Breakfast and dinner 7 days a week. BH asked much of that would JSS be willing to do? JSS confirmed his staff would be happy to serve the college. (BH) sent email requesting 3 company and 3 personal referrals. Sent three business references and four personal references, as requested, also provided banking contact to provide them with additional confidence.

03/01/11
- Got email w/picts from (BR) (Seagoville) on potential downtown site. Building "too new. Would have to change façade." (BR) has another building. Will contact JSS on 03/02 morning

03/02/11
- Received reply from (BH):"I apologize for the delay in getting back to you; I am waiting for approval from Mr. (G), (The IBLP president) on several things. The college has submitted 2 proposals and we have been working closely with that this week. Hope to talk with you by the end of today so we can move forward."
- Contacted by (KB) Exec. Assistant, Economic Development Corp. of Forney. Saw JSS on Good Morning Texas state that he was looking for a location in Seagoville. Viewed Crumbzz website. Said EDC Director would like us to preview Forney before

making any other decision. Checked out Forney (nice downtown. Rental on one unit (just rented) $XXXX per month. Gave her card. Will have someone call JSS. Didn't think there was anything available under 3,000 SQ FT.

- Met with (BR) (Seagoville) discussed possible sale of 104 N Kaufman. Also looked at residential home on edge of downtown (across from school). (BR) will Find out availability of house (may be too small) and asking price for 104 N. Kaufman. Will get back to JSS by 03/03/11
- Discussed Ambassador Park initial proposal with (BH): wants $XXX per week plus 1% of sale. Countered with $XXX per mo no % of sales. Also discussed College diner/breakfast plan. Suggested share % of revenue from college students. Run plan like a college meal plan. (BH) thinks they currently pay $4-6 per entree (includes 2-sides. Expect them to rent 40 rooms with 2-people per room (80 people min probably end up with 100 students. (BH) to get back with JSS on his proposal. JSS would love to bring life back to this grand old lady who has sat empty for years. Could feel the energy of the past staff in the kitchen bustling back and forth during her heyday. Re-using an old building and bringing it back to life fits perfectly with Crumbzz all natural, green, environmentally sound view!

03/04/11
- Received reply from with (BH) "Would like to offer our kitchen for lease to you for $XXXX per month which includes the storage space in the basement, kitchen, office, utilities, trash service, wireless internet. Want a 90-day trial period in which you and the Ministry Center have time to test our working relationship. If, for one reason or another the relationship is not working well at the end of this period, either or both of us would have the option of discontinuing the

working relationship. If it agrees with you we would like to waive the first month's rent in exchange for one of your delicious cake's a week for that month. After evaluating the first three months utility costs we can make adjustments if needed. I expect to have opportunities for catering meetings and events here at the center that would be available to you also. If you are in agreement with these terms and want to proceed please call me at XXX-XXX-XXXXor through email. We can also discuss the college meal plan once we decide the other. I look forward to talking with you and I am excited about the potential working with you. God Bless!

- Talked with (KB), Executive Director City of Forney Economic Development Corporation, regarding space in Forney. Provided www.crumbzz.com link as well as interview link. (KB) will review Crumbzz and get back to JSS to discuss availability of sites by end of day
- Set meeting with (KB) to view two properties in Forney on 03/09/11
- Discussed with (BR) of Seagoville the house (not available) and Insurance offices (City of Seagoville may subsidize part of rent). May set up time to view insurance offices (301 W. Malloy Bridge Road). Asked (BR) for address

03/08/11
- Discussed deal on Ambassador Park Hotel. JSS agreed to deal. JSS to start ASAP in kitchen.
- Met with (KB) and (DA) (Realtor) to view two properties in Forney. Store had issues with build out and cost $XXXX.
- (KB) found great old victorian house on Bois D Arc St. House rental was at $XXXX per mo. Told (KB) too expensive. Worked a very creative deal where we can share the building with The Art Commission of Forney and split rent/utilities. JSS wants build out paid by city. (DA) to find out if owner will allow the enclosing

of the side porch for storage. Owner will leave and even add all furniture with house. Kitchen needs hood oven range and grease trap. (KB) will find out what the city is willing to pay for. JSS to pay fort cost on all equipment and sundries.

03/11/11
- Moved equip. to Ambassador Park Hotel

03/12/11
- Updated and created 2nd set of recipe's for Ambassador

03/14/11
- Tested ovens (and updated recipe's) at Ambassador Hotel kitchen (cooked two cakes)
- Placed initial order (BEK) for stock at Ambassador Hotel kitchen

03/16/11
- Changed TX Sales & Use Tax Permit address to: 1312 South Ervay Street Dallas TX 75215 USA
- Picked up City of Dallas Registered Food Handler Certificate at: 7901 Goforth Road Dallas, TX75238 for the 1312 South Ervay Street Dallas, TX 75215 USA

PROJECT COMPLETED

Hire a Baker/Kitchen Manager/Sous Chef.
07/15/10
- Spoke w/(MC) of the (M Culinary Institute) regarding position. Set up meeting with (SVM) to discuss opportunity

07/30/10
- Met w/ (SVM) to discuss. Agreed on plan

08/23/10
- Met w/ (MC) to go over specifics of Crumbzz program

09/05/10
- (MC) decided not to participate

09/12/10
- Met w/ (SVM) regarding space and baker issue. (SVM) provided name of potential candidate (TC). (SVM)

also provided the name of a company that can bake the Crumbzz cake if needed (DC)

10/07/10
- Called (TC).
    - Discussed Crumbzz. She is taking care of her father would have to be part time during this time. Has extensive pastry chef background. Provided a brief overview of Crumbzz. Provided her with blog and website address. She will send resume
- Received resume

10/08/10
- Spoke with (SVM)
    - Updated her on Crumbzz status. Discussed conversation with (TC)

10/15/10
- Requested a meeting to discuss

10/21/10
- Received email from (TC); available 10/25-10/26.

Scheduled meeting 10/26/10 1 pm

10/25/10
- Met with (TC) to discuss Crumbzz (see below email:)
    - "I will continue to think about who might be good to be your bakery manager, and I have put a telephone call into my friend who has contacts in this field. He will contact you.

11/10/10
- Received an email from (ME) regarding position. Has an interest in baking for Crumbzz

11/15/10
- Will work hand-in-hand with JSS until JSS gets going. Once going would like to run kitchen. JSS concern about lack of material experience.

01/14/11
- Spoke with (MC) regarding Head Chef requirements. (MC) understands position and wants' to take

position. (MC) JSS will get back to her when a location has been settled on

03/08/11
- Spoke with (BH) of Ambassador Park Hotel (see Lock up site for cakes) he has a young man (LM), who has been to culinary school who is trying to come to America (from Philippines). If he has a committed job, he can get this work visa. He will live at hotel. (BH) will provide lodging and food for employee at hotel. (BH) will be visiting with candidate on 03/14-03/15. Will know at that time if he is a possible candidate. May have visa problems. JSS would love to help young man come to the U.S.

04/17/11
- Met with (LM):
- Provided NDA and No Compete to complete. Asked (LM) to review Crumbzz website and blog

05/18/11
- JSS started training (LM) Sous Chef who will work under him at the Ambassador kitchen.

PROJECT COMPLETED

Review the feasibility of opening a Crumbzz at DFW Airport Dallas

01/18/14
- Sent email to AirportInfoCenter @ dfwairport.com regarding a concession opportunity. Asked how to "Register" with DFW as a potential concessionaire.

01/21/14
- - 2:45 pm: Spoke to (D) gave JSS contact info for (MB) Assistant VP Concessions at DFW Airport.

01/21/14
- - 3:30 pm: Left voice mail with (MB) Assistant VP Concessions at DFW Airport regarding the possibility of Crumbzz adding a DFW concessionaire location.

01/23/14
- - 11:25 am: Called (D). Asked for additional contacts.

Provided JSS with: (ZC) VP Concessions 2200 South Service Road North Business Center 2nd Floor DFW Airport TX 75261; (MH) Assistant VP Concessions

02/07/14
- - 3:46 pm spoke to (MV) (ZC) assistant. Told JSS to register at XXXX also JSS to send email with Crumbzz info. 4:pm Submitted company space availability request registration (confirmation number 4407).

02/19/14
- Sent gift cake (Cinnamon Streusel), letter of introduction, Why DFW Brochure and Crumbzz Overview Brochure to (ZC)

03/27/14
- Spoke to (MV) (ZC) 's Assistant) re: to make sure they received the Crumbzz informational package and cake and to set up a meeting with (ZC) to discuss possible Crumbzz locations and to familiarize her with Crumbzz the company. (MV) stated that they did get the cake and package and it went quickly (NOTE: she did not have a taste. JSS will bring a piece to her when (if) he visits). (MV) will check with (ZC) and see if we can meet (or speak via phone) either 04/15/14 thru 04/17/14 or 04/22 thru 04/25/14. (MV) will call JSS back to confirm.

03/28/14
- (MV) set meeting for 04/15/13 1-pm - 1:45 pm, at DFW offices (2200 South Service Road, North Business Center, Second Floor, DFW Airport, TX 75261-9428). JSS to present to the following people: (ZC), (MB), (MM), (ML), (MV). Power Point or print presentation. Meetings usually lasts, 45 minutes to 1-hour. Prepared final PowerPoint and hand out presentations for review.

04/15/14
- Met with: (ZC), (MB), (MF). JSS presented Crumbzz story via Keynote presentation. Provided each participant with the Crumbzz Overview Brochure.

Served caramel sea salt cake. Provided several Minizz to (MB) to take home. Brought packaged cakes, Minizz and and party box of Minizz for presentation. Take away from presentation...Attendee's loved the Crumbzz idea, felt it definitely had a place at DFW, Bistro and Tasting Pavilions. Cautioned that there are challenges to getting in but if all are met, will do well in DFW. In addition, (ZV) suggested that we might want to consider offering our cakes through Host stores and other retailers at the airport as well. What the DFW team loved about Crumbzz: The product and packaging, That we are a local provider, Use of all natural ingredients, Our demographic target market is DFW Airport's demographic target market, We service business travelers, The two-sale idea of providing coffee/tea and slices of cakes for travelers as well as gift cakes to purchase and take on their trips to business meetings and family trips, We do PR on our story and company, D Terminal potential of the European dishes, Can use permanent spaces (European Bistro) or kiosk's (Tasting Pavilion), We were much more prepared than many other potential vendors, Will be on top of list of vendors wanting sites, However, JSS notes several challenges with operating at airport which include: Few available slots; Currently a lot of construction at most terminals; NOTE: Will be making more slots because of construction; Employee's must be approved (carded) by TSA; No local parking for employees (shuttle from satellite parking); Hours 6 am - 9 pm; Airport closings due to bad weather (may require being open for 24- hours per day until cleared out); NOTE: Upside to this issue - could be very lucrative; Challenges with getting approved to operate at airport include: Although we don't need to have it, ACDBE Certification is extremely helpful. This is a long a drawn out process. (ZC) suggested JSS contact (TL) Vice President Business and Diversity to move the process along ASAP. JSS called (TL) to set up meeting (left message).

04/23/14
- (TL) assistant called JSS to set up phone meeting. Meeting set for 9am 04/30/14

04/30/14
- JSS called (TL). Discussed Crumbzz potentially coming to DFW. Told her (ZC) requested (TL) contact (ZC) regarding Crumbzz. Wanted to fast track us into the airport. (TL) asked a few questions to make sure Crumbzz and JSS personally qualified.
- Is company solely owned (family business)
- Is personal net worth no more than $1.5 million (it is not)
- Is business annual gross more than $50 million (it is not) mSince Crumbzz qualifies on all the above counts. (TL) set up a meeting at DFW to have JSS present the company and then to move the program forward. Meeting is set for JSS to meet with (TL) Re; DFW ACDBE Certification. (TL) and her team will attend. JSS to make same presentation made with (ZC) and her team. Received invite from (JA) (TC assistant),. JSS accepted. Scheduled: May 16, 2014, 2:00:00 PM to 3:00:00 PM. Location: Admin Build. 3200 East Airfield Drive DFW Airport Texas 75261

05/16/14
- Met with: (TL) team (Vice President Business and Diversity, (SGS), (TG), (FG). JSS presented Crumbzz story via Keynote presentation. Provided each participant with the Crumbzz Overview Brochure. Served Cinnamon Streusel Cake. Brought packaged cake, Minizz and and Minizz party box for presentation. Take away from presentation... Attendee's loved the Crumbzz idea, felt it definitely had a place at DFW, Bistro and Tasting Pavilions. (TG) particularly impressed with Crumbzz. Said the new head of DFW visited European airports

and felt DFW was way behind on the upscale dining experiences. He felt Crumbzz would be exactly what this person would like. Will talk to (L) to get the ball rolling ASAP.

05/23/14
- Sent the following email to (TL) (copied all participants at the DFW meeting) (TL)- Thank you for allowing me to meet with your team, present the Crumbzz story and discuss the potential for Crumbzz locating one or more Crumbzz Bistro's and/or Tasting Pavilions at DFW International Airport. (SCS), (GT) and (FG) were most gracious hosts and extremely informative. We now have a pretty good idea of the upsides and challenges we will face moving forward. Since both parties feel Crumbzz would be a good fit at DFW, I would like to get the ball rolling on this program ASAP. Can you please provide us with the next steps on a moving forward plan to accomplish this goal. I hope you enjoyed the cake. Have a wonderful holiday. I look forward to speaking with you soon regarding the above.

05/23/14
- Received the following email from (TL) : "It was a pleasure meeting you. (FG) was kind enough to share the cake and it was one of the best I have tasted. (FG) is your point of contact and can assist you with next steps. Not sure where the two of you ended the conversation. I can step in wherever I am needed. Thanks"

6/10/14
- Contacted by (TL). DFW wants bistro's in every terminal (not just D terminal). JSS has a problem with opening bistro's (versus tasting pavilions) in all terminals. All dishes at the bistro's are made to order, this takes time and is not aligned well with travelers who are in a rush to catch a plane. JSS did not want to expose Crumbzz to the potential bad pr generated by

the time it would take to craft dishes. The tasting pavilions would only offer the cakes which would be available for consumption one premises as as gift cakes to take with travelers on their trips. These cakes, because they are made at Crumbzz bakery in Dallas and delivered daily, could be ready in ten minutes. (TL) stated that JSS could put a sign at each bistro stating the time issue. JSS did not want to deal with the potential downside of this. Decision was made to hold off from moving forward at this stage.

PROJECT COMPLETED

Review the feasibility of opening a Crumbzz in Downtown Dallas utilizing the Ground Floor Activation Program

01/23/14
- 10:30 am: Left voice mail with (DO) Business Network Manager, at (SL) regarding the possibility of Crumbzz adding a downtown Dallas location utilizing the Ground Floor Activation Program

01/23/14
- 10:35 am: Spoke to (ES) Senior Economic Development Coordinator regarding the above (see 01/23/14 - 10:30 am: (DO). Referred JSS to: (TL) Leak City of Dallas Senior Coordinator(214) (TL). (TL) is the person who runs the program. 01/23/14 - 10:50 am: Left voice mail for (TL). Briefly laid out Crumbzz and our intent to participate in the Ground Floor Activation Program. Provided www.Crumbzz.com internet address for her review.

02/04/14 -02/11/14 - 02/18/14
- Left voice mail for (TL) .

02/20/14
- Called (MD) (Senior Planner) Left voicemail. No return calls from (TL) . Asked for an alternate contact.

03/12/14
- Left a message on Mayor Mike Rawlings and Council

member Philip T Kingston's (downtown District 14 representative) emails: complaining about the lack of follow-up by (TL)

03/13/14
- Was copied on the following email from (CLS) Assistant to Philip T. Kingston Council District. (KZ), Good morning! Would you please have someone contact Mr. Sadler and let me know the outcome. Thanks. Email sent to:(KZ, KS, TL, PK, LH).

03/13/14
- Received a call from (TL) (Senior Coordinator) Apologized for delay in returning JSS call. Will send out info. on program. Received a copy of the Ground Floor Retail Activation Program Implementation of the program is not anticipated to begin until Spring of this year. I have your contact information and will add you to our list of potential program participants. (JH) in our office manages this program and I have provided his contact information below. JSS Called (JH) and spoke at length about the program and Crumbzz. Said program is expected to kick off in 05/14. Still negotiating with owners of buildings. He wants at least 6-month's and preferably a year of free rent so that companies can see if the market exists. Owners want 3-6 month's.(JH) previously lead the revitalization of downtown Plano. Will contact JSS when program up and running.

05/13/14
- JSS sent email to (JH).(JH)- regarding status of program. Received email reply from (JH); "We do not at this time have an official launch date as we are still finalizing the details to the program with our stakeholders. You are on our list of prospective tenants and I will keep you posted when the program is ready for launch.

06/1/14
- Called (JH) requesting update. Told JSS that program

is "all screwed up". Staff leaving, no one knows what's going on. Has no idea if and when it will EVER be activated.! JSS decided to drop out of consideration for a program and city that just doesn't have their act together.
PROJECT COMPLETED

Become a member of Forney Historic league (requirement under City of Forney contract with Crumbzz).
06/03/14
- Signed up as corporate member

PROJECT COMPLETED

Create commission schedule for commissioned sales force
05/28/14
- Set up sales commission program for Crumbzz sales force.

PROJECT COMPLETED

J Stephen Sadler

www.Sadler.media
www.JStephensGarden.com
www.Crumbzz.com

As an chef, restauranteur, epicurean travel host, FOX and CBS travel reporter, author and motivational speaker, J Stephen Sadler has a wide scope of experience in multiple fields.

A prolific best selling author, Sadler has authored a wide range of books that span multiple genre's from non-fiction memoirs (Quest For The Best), small business development (Bringing Fine Dining To Small Town America), world sourced recipes (The World On My Plate), to a delightful series of children's books (J Stephen's Garden – Happy Veggies Happy Garden Series).

His speaking engagements are as varied as his books. Although he is a sought after speaker on the corporate circuit for his motivational DISCovery seminars, Sadler does not limit his speaking engagements to the corporate world. His "I Can Eat That!" children's healthy eating presentations are a popular event at schools across the country and his "The Right Ingredient Can Make a World of a Difference" presentations are extremely popular at clubs and organizations.

CHILDREN'S BOOKS
J Stephen's Garden – Happy Veggies Happy Garden children's series of storybooks, coloring books and ebooks places its readers in the world of Farmer Bob and his family's encounters with the Veggies on their farm. Each of his storybooks features a delightful learning story of an individual veggie character who faces many of the challenges children face as they grow up. From being too short, the wrong color, different looking or simply too sad, each story teaches the reader that everyone is special in their own way. In addition, each book also includes a child-friendly recipe specifically made by the chef that the children can help make with their family. Readers will immediately identify with the challenges faced by Colinda Cauliflower, Bubba Broccoli, Chuckie Carrot, Eddie Eggplant, Sammy Spinach, Tanya Tomato, Paulina Potato and Sidney String Bean as they overcome their challenges, and find their special place in the world. His Children's books can be found on www.jstephensgarden.com and all online platforms and local retail outlets including: Amazon, Apple, Barnes & Noble, and Kobo.

NON-FICTION BOOKS
J Stephen Sadler's "Quest For The Best" documents his travels across the world in search of the finest culinary dishes culminating in a fascinating tour of the world of food through a restauranteur's eyes. It was a journey that began with his search for the origins of his family's 400 year old Crumbzz artisan crumb cake recipe. His story begins in a little town in Austria and continues as a quest to find the best of the best in

offerings from across the world! An absolute must reading for students of history, foodies and for those who believe that with the will, there is always a way. Quest For The Best can be purchased as a hardcover, paperback, ebook, and audio book and can be found on www.Sadler.media and all online platforms and retail outlets including: Amazon, Apple, Barnes & Noble, and Kobo.

The follow up to his original "Quest For The Best" book, Sadler's next book "Bringing Fine Dining To Small Town America" is a must read for small business entrepreneurs. Finding the right place to share his many world sourced recipes takes would be entrepreneurs on the challenges of not only finding the right location but also brand placement, packaging, site location and dealing with all the challenges of opening and maintaining a small bistro. Bringing Fine Dining To Small Town America is available in paperback and ebook and will be available on Amazon, Apple, Barnes & Noble, and Kobo, and local retail outlets.

Not wanting to limit his sharing of the wonderful recipes he had found during his travels, it was only natural that Chef J Stephen would craft an international recipe book. However, his "The World On My Plate" recipe book is not just a recipe book. Besides the fact that the book features not only every recipe featured in his bistros and those that never made it to prime time, the book also features the origins of all of the dishes, the secrets to using "the right ingredients" and even provides readers with a source guide on where to purchase the best of the best. My World On A Plate is available in hardback, paperback and ebook and will be available on Amazon, Apple, Barnes & Noble, and Kobo, and local retail outlets.

CHILDREN'S TOPICS - SPEAKING

J Stephens "I Can Eat That!" presentations are extremely popular with schools across the country. His child-friendly presentations encourage healthy eating in a form that children can not only easily understand but also presented in a form that has children going home and asking for his uniquely, child-friendly veggie dishes.

ADULT TOPICS - SPEAKING

J Stephen regularly speaks to groups interested in his areas of expertise. Traveling worldwide allows him to express his views of finding the best of the best in any business, small business branding and positioning, worldwide travel and utilizing his years of experience teaching the DISC personality profile system his DISCovery personal relationship building.

J Stephen is available to speak on all these topics and is happy to customize a keynote, workshop or discussion for your company, organization or group.

A few of his most popular topics include:

The Right Ingredient Is Not Always What You Think – Attendees learn that crafting a great dish is much more than simply following a recipe. Using the right ingredients can often be the difference between a so-so offering and a masterpiece. His worldwide travels in search of the finest ingredients provides a unique insight into what makes a dish special.

Who Am I, What Am I, Who Do I Serve – Deciding on your brand and positioning yourself or your company correctly in the marketplace can be the difference between success and failure. J Stephen's attention to the smallest details provides attendees with valuable tools that help businesses and individuals alike to separate themselves from all the noise.

DISCovery – J Stephen's experience utilizing the DISC Personality Identification System assists organizations in facilitating organizational change through personality awareness. His hands-on and online DISCovery seminars awaken participants to the discovery of their own personality types as well as the personalities of the people they work with, sell to, support and live with. Participants gain not only an awareness of their own personality traits but are also provided with invaluable tools on how best to identify and harmonize with those they interact with on a day-to-day basis.

To inquire about any of his speaking engagements visit www.Sadler.media or email: info@Sadler.media.

EPICUREAN GETAWAYS

Chef and world traveler J Stephen Sadler takes guests on a worldwide adventure visiting his personal favorite dining experiences in not only restaurants but also private homes around the world. A foodie and travel enthusiasts dream come true. Guests not only learn first hand where great food comes from but also how it is crafted and presented in exotic locations around the world. J Stephen's Gourmand Globe-Trotter Get-Aways allow travelers to experience the world of food one country at a time. To inquire about his Epicurean Getaways contact: info@Sadler.media.

RESTAURANTEUR

As a restauranteur, Mr Sadler leads Sadler Media in expanding the company's Crumbzz International Bistro concept and worldwide sales of the family Crumbzz artisan crumb cakes. His Crumbzz International Bistro features the many dishes he has procured from around the world. His artisan cakes are available on the Crumbzz website and are shipped worldwide to enthusiasts who value hand-crafted offerings, nestled in exquisite gift packaging. To inquire about his bistro and cakes, visit www.crumbzz.com.

SOCIAL MEDIA

Connect with J Stephen on social media at: Facebook, Twitter, LinkedIn, and Instagram: @jstephensadler

www.ingramcontent.com/pod-product-compliance
Lightning Source LLC
Chambersburg PA
CBHW050859240426
43673CB00026B/479/J